# WEDDING OF THE YEAR

## A Comedy

### NORMAN ROBBINS

SAMUEL           FRENCH

LONDON

NEW YORK   TORONTO   SYDNEY   HOLLYWOOD

MADE AND PRINTED IN GREAT BRITAIN BY
LATIMER TREND & COMPANY LTD PLYMOUTH

MADE IN ENGLAND

## CHARACTERS

**Ethel Murchinson**
**Peggy Ramskill**
**Walter Thornton**
**Frank Edwards**
**Alison Murchinson**
**Honoria Murchinson**
**Matilda Murchinson**
**Melvyn Thornton**
**Harry Elphinstone**
**Priscilla Edwards**

The action takes place in the living-room of the Murchinson home

ACT I
   Scene 1   Saturday morning
   Scene 2   That afternoon

ACT II
   Scene 1   That evening
   Scene 2   Saturday morning, six weeks later

Time—the present

## AUTHOR'S NOTE

Several years ago, when I was an amateur actor battling with my first leading role, a rather massive young lady many years my junior and playing my grandmother, remarked to me bitterly: "I wish someone would write a part for a fat girl and make *her* the lead. I never get a decent part in anything."

In more recent years, as a struggling Rep actor, the same remark was uttered to me by a pretty, but overweight, A.S.M. who seemed to spend her time making tea for the rest of us and playing maids and grandmothers.

When I announced my intention of writing a play and handing the leading role to a fat girl, almost everyone laughed. The two exceptions were myself and my wife Ailsa, who thinks me capable of anything.

Well—I've done it. All it needs now is for every fat girl in the country to demand the chance to play Alison and I'm convinced I'll be rich.

On a more practical note, however, I should just like to point out one thing. Alison is *not* as fat as she thinks she is. Her mode of dress simply adds to her dimensions. A normal girl wearing several sweaters of the woolly kind, or padding and a long skirt will create the illusion needed.

Finally, I would like to dedicate this play to my wife for all her advice and criticism during the writing of it, and to the St Giles Players of Pontefract for their patience and faith during long and tiresome rehearsals of all my plays.

Norman Robbins                                                    1976

# ACT I

## SCENE 1

*The living-room of the Murchinson home. Saturday morning*

*The room is a bright and cheerful one. Through an elegant arch at the back one can see into a hall and catch a glimpse of a staircase. A small table can be seen in the hall, and on it stands a beautiful bowl of dried flowers and ferns. On the wall behind this is an oval, gold-rimmed mirror, probably of good Victorian origin. A newly covered dining chair is situated at each side of the arch—one of these has a rip-off seat for use with Velcro tape. Two more doors give access to the room—one to the parlour and one to the kitchen. Between them is the fireplace, a neat, modern type, dotted with ornaments. Over it hangs an oval mirror. Opposite, a large picture window looks out over a small, neatly kept garden and the street. Spotless net curtains and brocade drapes hang. A framed print of an Old Master hangs on the wall above a drop-leaf table. The floor is richly carpeted throughout. (For furniture see the plan on p. 78)*

*When the* CURTAIN *rises, the sun is streaming through the window, the fire is lit, and the room is empty. A cup, saucer and plate of assorted biscuits are on the coffee-table. After a slight pause, Ethel Murchinson enters from the kitchen. She is a pleasantly plump woman of about forty-five, neatly dressed and carrying a silver coffee-pot. She goes to the coffee-table to pour herself a cup, singing softly to herself as she does so*

**Ethel** (*singing*) This is my lovely day. This is the day I shall remember the day I'm dying. La, la de da de da. De da de something, something de da da, seabirds crying . . .
**Peggy** (*off*) Oo—oo! Anybody home?
**Ethel** (*calling*) Through here, Peggy. (*She puts the coffee-pot down*)

*Peggy Ramskill enters from the hall. She is a slim-built woman of about Ethel's age. She is dressed in a very smart outfit, obviously new, and her hair is elegantly styled. She poses in the doorway*

**Peggy** (*imitating a trumpet call*) Tarraaaaaa! (*She moves down to meet Ethel*) What do you think to it? (*She parades the dress*)
**Ethel** (*admiringly*) Oh, Peggy. It's lovely.
**Peggy** I thought you'd like it. It's only a copy, worse luck, but I just had to buy *something* or I'd have gone mad.
**Ethel** (*with a smile*) Why? What's to do? No . . . hold on. I'll get another cup first.

*Ethel exits to the kitchen*

**Peggy** (*sitting on the sofa*) Have you seen the paper this morning, Ethel?
**Ethel** (*off*) Local or national?
**Peggy** (*helping herself to a biscuit*) Local, of course. Who reads the nationals these days? There's nothing in them but wars and riots, and how many times Princess Anne's fallen off her horse. Complete waste of money if you ask me.

*Ethel enters with a cup and saucer*

**Ethel** Well the answer's no to both. I haven't had time to look at a paper today. This is the first break I've had since I got our Frank off to work this morning. (*She puts the things down on the coffee-table*)
**Peggy** (*finishing her biscuit*) What's he doing working on a Saturday?
**Ethel** (*pouring*) Trying to keep in front of the Tax man, I expect. How should I know? Anyway, never mind about *him*. What's with *you* and this new outfit? (*She sits beside Peggy*)
**Peggy** (*pulling a face*) Depression.
**Ethel** (*surprised*) You? Since when?
**Peggy** (*taking her coffee*) Since I looked at the *Weekly Journal* this morning. (*She takes another biscuit*) You remember I told you I'd sent the details of our Edna's wedding into them? For their "Bride of the Year" competition?
**Ethel** Yes.
**Peggy** Well, I was convinced they'd choose *her*. After all—we're not exactly nobodies around here—me and Phil—are we? And it's going to be the biggest wedding *this* town's seen for a good many years, I can tell you. Oh, yes. Not to mention the fact that Jeremy happens to be their Assistant Advertising Manager, as well. It stood to reason they'd choose one of their own staff as winner, didn't it? Well, that's what *we* thought, anyway.
**Ethel** But they haven't?
**Peggy** (*disgusted*) No. It's in this morning's paper. We didn't even get a look in. And you'll never guess who *did* win it.
**Ethel** I've no idea.
**Peggy** Mary Turnbull and that coloured chap she's marrying. Assam Whatsisname. What do you think of *that*?
**Ethel** Well—I don't know. What *should* I think?
**Peggy** (*bridling*) Well, it's a bit *off*, isn't it? I mean if she wants to marry a coloured chap, that's her own lookout, isn't it? But he's not been in the town two minutes, and it makes my blood boil to think of him walking off with that two hundred pounds and a free honeymoon in Paris. You'd have thought they'd at least have picked an English couple to give the money to, wouldn't you? Somebody who could have done with it, instead of somebody who's rolling in it already.
**Ethel** (*playing it down*) Well—it would have been just the same if your Edna had won it, wouldn't it, now?

**Peggy** (*puzzled*) How do you mean?

**Ethel** Well, you're not exactly *destitute*, are you?

**Peggy** (*still smarting*) Maybe we're not—but we've had to work damned hard for what we've got. Me and my Phil. It makes me see red. I've been telling *everybody* our Edna was going to win that competition and I shall feel a right fool, now.

**Ethel** Never mind, Peggy. It'll soon blow over.

**Peggy** That's not the point, Ethel. I feel *cheated*. Jeremy Phillips almost *promised* me our Edna's wedding would win that prize. (*She sniffs*) You can't rely on *anybody* these days, can you? It makes me wonder just what sort of a husband she's let herself in for, when something like this happens.

**Ethel** You can hardly blame Jeremy for it, Peggy. It wouldn't be *his* fault. Perhaps the editors felt that it might cause talk if one of their own people won.

**Peggy** (*tartly*) It'll certainly cause talk tonight when he comes round to take her out. She'll be *furious*. She was counting on that money for spending.

**Ethel** (*lifting the coffee-pot*) More coffee?

**Peggy** No thanks. I'll have to cut down on milky drinks. I'm starting to spread in the middle again. (*She sighs*) You don't know how lucky you are, Ethel, not having to worry about your figure. *I* have to count every calorie.

**Ethel** I didn't notice you counting the ones in the biscuits. And anyway— what makes you think I don't have to worry about *my* figure? (*She pours herself more coffee*)

**Peggy** Because I've known you too long. You've always been on the plump side, haven't you? You were a real little tubby even before you had your Alison, and you certainly haven't got smaller since. You know—she must have got it from *you*, because she certainly didn't get it from Stan, did she? He was as thin as a rake.

**Ethel** (*glancing down*) No—she doesn't take after Stan.

**Peggy** It's a pity he didn't live to see her married. I know he'd have liked to.

**Ethel** (*quietly*) Yes. He wanted to see her wed.

**Peggy** I don't suppose *you'd* mind, either, would you? It's about time she did. I mean—you'd have thought she'd have been able to find *somebody* who'd have her, but she doesn't seem to mind at all, does she? I know when I was her age, I'd have been worried stiff if some young fellow hadn't been chasing me from dawn to dusk. Not that I ever had any worries in *that* direction. Quite the opposite, in fact. (*Smugly*) My problem was how to get rid of them.

**Ethel** (*wryly*) Yes, I remember.

**Peggy** (*laughing*) I used to palm them off in your direction, didn't I?

**Ethel** And they'd take one look at me, then run for their lives.

**Peggy** Still—you didn't miss much, Ethel. They were all the same when you got down to it. So slow you wanted to scream . . . or so fast you *had* to. (*She laughs at the memory*)

**Ethel** I struck lucky in the end though, didn't I? With Stan. He was well worth waiting for. (*She smiles*) Perhaps our Alison's waiting for *her* Stan to come along.

**Peggy** He'll have to get a move on then if he's going to. What is she now? Twenty-two? Three?

**Ethel** Twenty-three.

**Peggy** Well, never mind. Perhaps she'll meet somebody one day who's a bit short sighted, and the wedding bells'll start ringing for them. You can always live in hope, can't you? (*She rises*) I'll have to be going, I suppose. Thanks for the coffee.

**Ethel** (*her thoughts elsewhere*) Any time.

**Peggy** I'll see myself out. I think I know the way by now.

**Walter** (*off*) Are you there, Ethel?

**Ethel** (*rising*) Come in, Walter. (*To Peggy*) It's Walter Thornton from next door. He'll have brought the flowers for Aunt Cilla. He does it every Saturday.

*Walter Thornton enters from the hall. He is a man of about fifty, casually dressed and carrying a bunch of flowers*

**Walter** (*seeing Peggy*) Oh—sorry. I didn't realize you had company.

**Ethel** (*moving to him*) Come in, Walter. (*She leads him down to Peggy*) This is Peggy. Peggy Ramskill. An old schoolfriend of mine. Peggy— Walter Thornton.

**Walter** (*holding his hand out to shake*) How do you do?

**Peggy** (*with a huge smile*) Hello. (*She pumps his hand*)

**Walter** (*to Ethel*) I've brought the flowers. (*He shows them*)

**Ethel** Oh, they're beautiful, Walter.

**Walter** I'm sorry there's not more, but Melvyn's been at it again. These are all I've managed to save.

**Ethel** Oh, what a shame.

**Peggy** I know *just* how you feel, Mr Thornton. Our Rex is always burying his bones in the middle of the rose beds.

**Ethel** (*laughing*) Melvyn's not a dog, Peggy. He's Walter's son.

**Peggy** Oh. (*Embarrassed*) I'm ever so sorry.

**Walter** You're not half as sorry as me. I've got to live with him.

**Ethel** (*reprovingly*) Oh, come on, Walter. He's not as bad as that.

**Walter** No—he's worse. There's only him would try to mow the lawn with hair clippers and a vacuum cleaner.

**Peggy** (*amused*) What?

**Walter** He thought it'd save him the bother of raking up the bits after-wards. All he succeeded in doing was clogging up the motor and taking the heads off my prize blooms.

**Ethel** (*upset*) Oh, Walter. (*Taking the flowers*) Still—I suppose he meant well—as usual. And *these* are beautiful. I'll just take them up to Aunt Cilla.

**Walter** You can tell her I might have some roses for her next week— unless he starts breeding greenfly.

*Ethel laughs and exits up the stairs*

*Peggy and Walter look at each other and smile shyly*

**Peggy** (*suddenly, after a long pause*) I—er—I've not seen you round here before, have I?

**Walter** No.

**Peggy** It's just that I seem to *know* you from somewhere.

**Walter** Oh, well, you've probably seen me knocking about the town sometime. I'm out and about most days.

**Peggy** Yes. I suppose that's it. Although I don't get round here myself all that much. Just when I'm in the district. (*Pause*) We live the other side, you see. Hillingdon.

**Walter** Oh. Nice area.

**Peggy** (*smugly*) That's what *we* think. Phil and me. (*She smiles*) Phil's my husband.

**Walter** (*with a slight frown*) Not Phil Ramskill who runs that big electrical shop in Hagley Street?

**Peggy** (*pleased*) That's right. Do you know Phil, then? (*She preens*)

**Walter** Know him? I'll say I know him. He's the biggest swindler this side of the Pennines.

**Peggy** (*startled*) I beg your pardon.

**Walter** (*annoyed*) Charged me twenty-five pence for a fitting I could have got in Woolworth's for half the price.

**Peggy** (*tartly*) Well, in that case, Mr Thornton, I suggest you go to Woolworth's in future. It so happens we have a lot of very high overheads on those premises, and the money's got to come from somewhere.

**Walter** That's as maybe—but it's not going to come from *me*, thank you very much.

**Peggy** (*furiously*) We should have to close down if we had to rely on people like you to keep us going. One light fitting and a couple of batteries a year, and you think you're doing us a favour. Well, let me tell you, Mr Thornton—we can do very well *without* your favours.

**Walter** It's a damn good job you can, Missis, because you won't be getting any more of 'em.

*Ethel enters down the stairs, all smiles*

**Ethel** Now then. How are you two getting on?

**Peggy** (*snapping*) We're not.

**Ethel** (*startled*) Pardon? (*She looks quickly at them both*)

**Peggy** I've never been so insulted in my life as I have been this morning in this house. This "friend" of yours has just had the nerve to accuse my Phil of overcharging him in the shop.

**Ethel** (*to Walter*) Oh, you must be mistaken . . .

**Walter** There's no mistake. It's no wonder they can afford to live in Hillingdon the prices he charges. They'll be moving into Windsor Castle next.

**Peggy** (*to Ethel*) I think I'd better go before I say something I might regret later.

**Ethel** Peggy . . .

**Peggy** (*forcing a smile*) Don't worry, Ethel, I'm not blaming *you*. I can't hold you responsible for your friends and their lack of manners. I'll see you next week, perhaps? (*To Walter*) Good morning, Mr Thornton. (*She moves up to the arch then turns*) And I hope that the next time we're expected to meet . . . we won't.

*Peggy exits through the hall*

**Ethel** (*upset*) Oh, Walter. What was all that about? What did you say?

**Walter** (*slightly embarrassed*) Oh—I just mentioned that her precious husband had overcharged me for a light fitting I put up when we first moved in next door. It was only a storm in a teacup. Nothing to get excited about.

**Ethel** (*sighing*) Oh, well—I expect she'll get over it. Sit down, and I'll get you a cup of coffee—or would you prefer tea?

**Walter** (*sitting on the sofa*) I'm easy. Coffee'll do. Er . . . what did the old lady think to the flowers?

**Ethel** (*moving to the kitchen door*) She loved them, of course. I put them on her dressing-table so she can see them without any difficulty. It really makes her day when you bring those flowers, you know. If only you could see her face when I take them in.

*Ethel exits to the kitchen*

**Walter** (*slightly louder*) Well, it can't be much fun for her, lying up there, month in and month out, can it? If a few flowers can brighten her life up, well—there's always a bunch in my garden.

*Ethel enters with a cup and saucer*

**Ethel** It is good of you, Walter. (*She goes to the coffee-table*)

**Walter** Has there been any improvement in her?

**Ethel** (*pouring*) How do you mean?

**Walter** Getting any better, like?

**Ethel** (*blankly*) Better? (*She realizes*) Oh—no. No.

**Walter** (*gravely*) Sorry to hear it.

**Ethel** There's nothing wrong with her. (*She hands him the cup*)

**Walter** (*startled*) Eh?

**Ethel** You didn't think she was ill, did you? (*She laughs*) Good heavens no. There's nothing wrong with Aunt Cilla but *boredom*. She could come down those stairs this very minute if she thought there'd be something for her to stick her nose into, but there isn't, so there she stays. (*Sitting beside Walter*) Besides, she keeps telling us it'll save the bother of having to carry her upstairs when she finally drops dead.

**Walter** You mean—she just lays there and lets you run up and down them stairs, wearing yourself out, while she pretends to be bed-ridden? Well, by heck.

**Ethel** She does nothing of the sort, Walter Thornton, and besides, she looks after Alison.

**Walter** Alison? But the lass is nearly twenty-four.

**Ethel** I know. But you know what she's like. People can be very cruel when a girl's her size. Oh, I'm not saying they mean it, but she gets herself into a state about it at times, and—well—Aunt Cilla's a wonderful help to her. Makes her see the funny side of it and all that. I mean—she *knows* she's big, Walter, but she doesn't want reminding about it every two minutes. That's why I'm so grateful to Aunt Cilla. She's got the knack of knowing just how to handle her when she's feeling low.

**Walter** Aye. (*Pause*) You—er—you don't think she could manage to find room for one more up there, do you? (*Quickly*) Oh, I'm not meaning me. I can look after myself. I'm thinking of our Melvyn.

**Ethel** (*laughing*) Walter.

**Walter** No, I'm serious. He could do with somebody to talk a bit of sense into him before he manages to kill somebody with them crackpot inventions of his.

**Ethel** Oh, go on with you. He's not half as bad as you make him out to be. Now come on. Admit it.

**Walter** I'm admitting nothing. What about the time he got the bright idea of fitting the house up with central heating? And ended up by blowing up half the front room and landing?

**Ethel** Well—that *was* unfortunate, I admit—but I blame the Gas Board, myself. They should never have put their pipes so close to the water ones.

**Walter** (*disgusted*) Shattered every window in the street, that blast did—and blew old Sally Wilkinson head first into her own compost heap. (*Warming to the subject*) And look at that paint he mixed up to do the garden shed with. Still not dry—and it's two years ago last August since he painted it. Anyway—I've not come round here to moan about him, have I? So I'll shut up.

**Ethel** What *did* you come round for? Besides to bring the flowers?

**Walter** And upset your friend.

**Ethel** (*wryly*) And that.

**Walter** Well—I just wondered if you'd be interested in coming out for a drive this afternoon. A little trip into the country?

**Ethel** Oh, Walter. I'd love to.

**Walter** Good.

**Ethel** But I can't. The Aunts are coming to see Cilla. I *am* sorry, but I've just got to be here to make the tea and things. (*Pause*) How about *next* week? Or wouldn't that be convenient for you?

**Walter** (*pleased*) Any time's convenient for me. We'll make it a date, then?

**Ethel** (*smiling*) It's a date. And I'll look forward to it.

**Walter** Me an' all. (*He stands*) Well, I'd best be off and see if the house is still standing. Thanks for the coffee.

**Ethel** (*rising*) Thank *you* for the flowers.
**Walter** It's a pleasure. (*He glances upwards*) Boredom. (*He laughs*) I'll
bring you the flowers round next Saturday as usual. Bye.

*Walter exits through the hall*

*Ethel smiles and begins to clear the coffee cups*

*Alison Murchinson and Frank Edwards enter through the hall. Alison is a
pleasant, over-fat girl of twenty-three, wearing a shapeless coat over an
over-large sweater and heavy skirt. She wears comfortable flat shoes, has
long straight hair, and wears pebble-glass spectacles. Frank is thirty-five,
slim and good-looking. He is dressed in oil-stained overalls, and carries
a lunch-box and a wrapped box of chocolates*

**Frank** (*as he enters*) I'm back, Sis. (*He puts the lunch-box on the sofa*)
**Ethel** (*surprised*) It's not *that* time, is it? (*She glances at her watch*) I've
hardly had time to turn round.

*Alison removes her coat behind the sofa*

Hello, love.
**Frank** Been having another coffee morning, then?
**Ethel** No. Just Peggy and Mr Thornton. (*She gathers up everything but the
biscuits and moves kitchenwards*)
**Alison** (*draping her coat on the sofa*) Are those biscuits spare, Mum?
**Ethel** (*at the door*) Alison . . .
**Alison** Well—I'm hungry. (*She takes two*) It's nearly an hour since I ate last.
**Frank** Poor love. She's going to drop dead of starvation in a minute.
Collapse on the carpet and expire—all fifty-four stone of her.
**Alison** Stinker. (*She plonks herself on the sofa, just missing the lunch-box*)
**Frank** Careful. You know we've got dry rot under that.
**Ethel** (*smiling*) Oh, let her alone, Frank. I'll go and make a few sand-
wiches for you both.
**Frank** Not for me, thanks. I've not finished all the others.

*Alison eagerly opens the lunch-box and takes out the sandwiches inside it*

Besides—I'd hate to deprive her of another pound of fat.
**Ethel** (*warningly*) Frank.
**Alison** (*munching*) I don't mind, Mum. He can say what he likes about me.
I'd much rather be nice and cuddly than as thin as a stick of spaghetti
like him.

*Ethel shakes her head and exits into the kitchen*

**Frank** Ha—listen to the child. (*He puts the chocolates on the drop-leaf
table*)
**Alison** Not so much of the child, Grand-dad. You're only ten years older
than I am. (*She munches happily on a sandwich*)

*Ethel enters and goes to the sofa for Alison's coat*

**Frank** Twelve, actually—but I *am* ten stone lighter. How you ever expect a knight in shining armour to come along and carry *you* off, I can't imagine. He'd never be able to lift you.

**Alison** With a face like mine, he'd have to be a blind navvy with a fork-lift truck. (*She takes a biscuit*)

**Ethel** (*holding the coat*) Don't be silly, Alison. There's nothing wrong with your face.

**Frank** Well—nothing that a good black-out couldn't fix. (*He grins*)

**Ethel** (*crossly*) Now stop it, Frank.

**Alison** (*unconcerned*) Oh, it's all right, Mum. Besides—he's right, isn't he? With my looks, if I were being threatened by a dragon, and a knight in shining armour came riding by—he'd slay me and ride off into the sunset with the dragon. (*She takes another biscuit*)

**Frank** And I should think so, too. There's far too much indiscriminate slaying of dragons, these days. One of these mornings we'll be waking up and finding out that there's none left. (*He begins to sit in the easy chair*)

**Ethel** (*spotting him*) Ahhhhh! Not in your overalls, Frank Edwards. Not on my clean covers. (*She pushes him away*) You can go upstairs and change while I get the lunch under way. (*She takes the coat out into the hall to hang it*)

**Alison** And don't forget the sandwiches, Mum.

**Frank** (*moving to the arch*) Oh, by the way, Sis. There's a box of chocs on the table there.

**Ethel** (*returning*) Oh, Frank. You shouldn't have done.

**Frank** I didn't. They're the ones you ordered for Aunt Pris from Mrs Shepherd.

*Frank pulls a face at Ethel, laughs, and exits through the hall*

**Ethel** Honestly. (*She shakes her head*) I suppose you'll be wanting a drink as well, young lady?

**Alison** (*nodding*) Please. But I'll have the sandwiches first. Want a hand?

**Ethel** No, thank you. Stay where you are. I'll do it.

**Alison** (*pleading*) You won't be too long, will you? I'm starving.

**Ethel** (*sighing*) Two minutes.

*Ethel shakes her head and exits to the kitchen*

**Alison** (*calling*) Extra thick ones, please. With pickle. (*She rises and moves over to the drop-leaf table, picks up the chocolates, looks at them, grimaces and replaces them. She then moves over to the window to peer out, singing softly*) Food, glorious food. Spuds, roast beef and mustard. While I'm still in the mood. Suet pudding and custard . . . (*She turns away from the window and picks up a magazine from the top of the bookcase, flicking through the pages*) Roast chickens and casseroles—this week's patterns for knitting. More letters to Evelyn Home . . . (*She stops singing and reads out aloud*) "Slim your way to happiness." (*She sits on the sofa again*) "Linda Oliphant was eighteen stone seven pounds before she began our special diet. Now, only ten weeks later, she is down to a trim fifteen stone four. How did this miracle occur? Let Linda tell you in her own words." Huh. Same old rubbish.

*Frank enters from the hall in slacks and sweater*

**Frank** What is?

**Alison** (*glumly*) Dieting.

**Frank** (*groaning*) Not again. I couldn't stand it. (*He goes to the easy chair*) I still remember the last one you tried. What was it? A raw carrot and a glass of water a day, or something.

**Alison** (*nodding*) And what happened? I put five pounds *on*. (*She sighs*) If only there were a *foolproof* way of losing weight. You know. Without having to starve yourself to death to do it.

**Frank** (*sitting*) There *is*. You can lose two stone in a couple of hours these days—if you can afford it.

**Alison** (*amazed and interested*) How?

**Frank** Have a leg amputated. (*He grins*)

**Alison** (*furiously*) Pig. (*She throws the magazine at him*)

**Frank** (*dodging it*) That's no way to speak to your uncle, young lady.

**Alison** Well—stop pulling my leg then.

**Frank** Pulling it? I couldn't even lift it. (*He looks around*) Where's the paper?

**Alison** Toilet, wall or news?

**Frank** Ho ho. And who's been in the knifebox today, then? The *Journal*, of course.

**Alison** (*shrugging*) No idea.

**Frank** Be a love and find it for me.

**Alison** What did your last slave die of?

**Frank** Finding newspapers. Go on. I've been working all morning.

**Alison** (*rising*) Playing cards, more like.

**Frank** Do you *mind*? We don't have time to play cards at our place.

**Alison** (*in mock surprise*) Really? How much did you lose?

**Frank** I didn't. I won thirty pence.

*They both laugh*

**Alison** Does that mean you'll be able to take me out to dinner tonight? Or will you be taking Sexy Sally from the tobacconists?

**Frank** (*amused*) You mean the suicide blonde piece behind the sweet counter? Do me a favour. She must be sixty if she's a day.

**Alison** There's many a good tune played on an old fiddle.

**Frank** And there's only snow on the roof when the fire's out.

*They both laugh*

**Alison** (*giggling*) You know—we're getting as bad as the Aunts.

**Frank** (*with a loud mock groan*) Oh, don't.

**Alison** I wonder what new gems they'll have in store for us today?

**Frank** (*sitting up*) Eh? They're not coming round *today*, are they?

**Alison** First Saturday in the month.

**Frank** Oh, well. That settles it. I'm going out. I can't take any more. My nerves won't stand it.

**Alison** (*consoling him*) Poor delicate thing. (*She raps him on the head*) I'll go and find you that paper.

*Alison exits to the parlour. Ethel enters with a plate of sandwiches and takes them to the coffee-table*

**Ethel** Sandwiches. Tea'll be ready in a minute. Where's Alison?

**Frank** Looking for the *Journal*.

**Ethel** It's upstairs. Aunt Cilla's got it.

*Alison returns*

**Alison** It's not in there.

**Frank** (*indicating the ceiling*) We've been beaten to it by the Lady of the Camellias.

**Ethel** I'll go see if she's finished with it. She only wants to see the obituary notices in case she knows someone.

**Alison** It's all right. I'll go. (*She sees the sandwiches*) Ah, food. My favourite sort. (*She takes two*)

**Frank** Edible ones.

**Alison** Must feed a growing girl. (*She moves up to the arch*)

**Frank** The only growing you're doing is outwards.

*Alison cocks a snook at him*

**Ethel** Oh, Alison. You can take that box of chocolates up as well, if you don't mind.

**Frank** And don't scoff them before you get to the top of the stairs.

**Alison** As if I would. And besides—they're all ginger and I don't like it.

*Alison picks up the chocolates and exits upstairs*

**Frank** At last—something she *doesn't* like. Hold me up.

**Ethel** Frank.

**Frank** You know—it's no wonder she hasn't managed to get herself married off. The chap'd have to be earning a fortune to keep her in food.

**Ethel** (*prodding him*) You've some need to talk, Frank Edwards. I haven't noticed *you* breaking your neck to coax some poor unsuspecting female into matrimony.

**Frank** Ah—well. That's different, isn't it? I'm choosey, you see.

**Ethel** Meaning Alison shouldn't be, I suppose?

**Frank** I didn't say that. Anyway, it's different for a man, Sis. It doesn't matter to us about settling down. But *look* at her. You couldn't ask for a nicer girl, could you? Intelligent. Kind. And I'm not saying that because of you. If she weren't my own niece I'd marry her myself. But with a figure like that, what chap's going to look at her twice . . . unless it's to check that his eyes aren't playing him tricks. Why don't you make her see a *doctor* about it?

*Alison appears on the staircase and comes down to the arch, unseen by them*

She's getting so fat now, by the time she's thirty she'll probably explode.
**Ethel** Frank . . . (*She sits on the sofa*)
**Frank** I'm sorry, Sis, but you'll have to do *something* about it, you really will.

*Alison moves into a hidden position*

**Ethel** (*distressed*) What *can* I do, Frank? She's tried dieting *hundreds* of times. You know she has. And nothing seems to make any difference. She's just given up the struggle.
**Frank** But she can't afford to. Not if she doesn't want to remain single all her life.
**Ethel** (*with a sigh*) I know . . .
**Frank** Then you've got to make her see *reason*. Tell her she *must* get rid of all that flab or she'll never get herself a husband. And it might help if she got herself some contact lenses and got rid of those specs.
**Ethel** (*worried*) It's all very well you sitting there and saying all this—but what can I say to her so that I don't sound—well—you know?
**Frank** Hang it all, Sis, you are her mother. (*Pause*) Would you like me to . . .?
**Ethel** (*quickly*) No. No. I'll do it, Frank. I'll do it.
**Frank** I *am* right, Ethel, aren't I? (*He rises and moves to her*)
**Ethel** (*looking down*) I suppose so.
**Frank** I wouldn't hurt her feelings for the world. You know that—but if she's not careful, she'll—well—she'll just . . .
**Ethel** End up on the shelf?
**Frank** (*touching her shoulder*) If they can build one strong enough to support her. (*He grins*)
**Ethel** (*smiling wanly*) All right, Frank. I'll try and say something to her later. I'd best go and make that tea now. The kettle will be boiling it's head off.
**Alison** (*off, singing*) On a wonderful day like today . . . (*She comes down with a paper*) One paper, your lordship. (*She tosses it to him*)
**Ethel** (*rising*) I'm just going to bring in the tea. Don't forget to leave some sandwiches for Frank, will you?
**Alison** He—er—he can have what's left. I—er—I've had enough, thanks.

*Frank and Ethel exchange surprised glances*

**Frank** (*moving back to the armchair*) Good heavens. The child's refusing food. (*To Alison*) Do you feel all right?
**Alison** Perfectly, thank you. (*She sits on the sofa*)

**Frank** (*in mock astonishment*) You don't mean to tell me you're full? (*He sits*) Wonders will never cease.

**Alison** (*haughtily*) Some of us *do* know when to stop, Mr Edwards.

**Ethel** (*smiling*) She doesn't want to spoil her appetite for lunch, do you, love?

**Alison** Oh—I—er—I won't be in for lunch today, Mum. I've just remembered. I promised to meet Mavis Todd in town. We—we're going to the Chinese restaurant.

**Frank** I'd better phone them up and let them know you're coming. They can get an extra barge-load of rice on the boil.

**Alison** Fried chopsticks to you.

*Ethel smiles and exits into the kitchen*

**Frank** (*opening the paper*) And now for a quick look at the local scandal.

**Alison** Don't forget to check if they've spelled your name right.

**Frank** Ho, ho, ho. (*He holds the paper up in front of his face and reads*)

*Alison stares at the back of the paper, and without thinking, reaches out for a sandwich. She is about to pop it into her mouth when she realizes what she is doing and quickly drops it back on to the plate*

**Alison** Frank . . .

**Frank** Hmmm?

**Alison** Is it true about your friend designing the wedding dress for Mary Turnbull?

**Frank** (*without looking up*) You mean Harry? Harry Elphinstone?

**Alison** That's him.

**Frank** Yes, why?

**Alison** Nothing. (*Pause*) Lucky thing. Wish he'd design one for me. I don't suppose he's done a bell-tent before, has he?

**Frank** (*looking up*) Sorry?

**Alison** She's going to be "Bride of the Year", isn't she? Mary Turnbull.

**Frank** That's what the paper says.

**Alison** I suppose they've got her picture in there, as well, haven't they?

**Frank** I wouldn't know. (*He carries on reading*)

**Alison** I bet they have.

**Frank** (*sighing*) Meaning you want to have a look, I suppose? (*He turns over the pages*) Yes—here she is. Page seven.

**Alison** (*going to him to look*) Huh. She doesn't look particularly pretty, does she?

**Frank** Me—owwwwww.

**Alison** Oh, shut up. She's got almost as many chins as I have.

**Frank** Impossible.

*Alison slaps him lightly on top of the head*

Owww!

**Alison** Serves you right for being cheeky to me. Next time I'll *sit* on you.

**Frank** (*in mock horror*) Mercy.

*Ethel enters with tea things and puts them on the coffee-table*

**Ethel** Now what are you up to?

**Alison** Looking at this picture of Mighty Mary. The village belle; champion lady wrestler—and this year's blushing bride.

**Ethel** Alison . . . (*She pours the tea*)

**Alison** Sorry. Still—at least it isn't pasty-faced Edna Ramskill they've chosen, is it? I couldn't have stood that.

**Frank** Is *she* getting married as well?

**Alison** Oh, yes. Everybody's getting married but me.

**Frank** I'm not surprised. They'd never be able to get you through the church doors.

**Ethel** (*sharply*) Now stop it, Frank.

**Frank** Can you imagine it, though? Sixteen all-in wrestlers trying to force her inside, and the organist playing "Here comes the Bride—all fat and wide". (*He laughs*)

*Alison grabs the paper and beats him over the head with it, laughing. He howls in mock pain*

**Ethel** (*amused*) Now stop it, you two. Alison—give over. I've not read that paper yet.

**Alison** (*dropping the paper in Frank's lap*) It's a good job I'm only a fragile blossom, or he'd have known about it, just then.

**Ethel** Come on. Get this tea before it gets cold. How many sandwiches do you want, Frank? (*She picks up a cup of tea for him*)

*Alison returns to the sofa*

**Frank** How many are left?

**Alison** Not many. (*She takes one*)

**Frank** I thought you weren't hungry?

*Ethel takes the plate to him and he helps himself. Alison sits on the sofa to drink her tea and eat. There is a chime of bells from the front door*

**Ethel** (*to Alison*) See who that is, love, will you?

**Frank** If it's the Aunts, give me a yell, and I can get out before they see me.

**Ethel** Honestly, Frank . . .

*Alison exits to the front door*

**Frank** Sorry, Sis, but you know I can hardly keep my face straight whenever they're around. I bet they even sign their letters "Proverbially yours".

**Ethel** (*chuckling*) Well, you needn't worry yourself. They aren't due for at least another two hours, so you can finish eating your sandwich. I expect it'll be the milkman or something.

*Alison enters*

**Alison** It's Mrs Ramskill.

*Peggy enters behind Alison, a look of great excitement on her face*

**Peggy** Ethel—have you *heard*?
**Ethel** (*blankly*) Heard?
**Peggy** (*gleefully*) It's off.

*Alison, Frank and Ethel look at one another*

The *wedding*.
**Ethel** You mean your Edna and Jer . . .
**Peggy** (*impatiently*) No, you dope. Mary Turnbull's. It's off. She's not getting married after all. I've just heard about it.
**Ethel** (*bewildered*) But why? I mean—what's happened?
**Peggy** (*taking a deep breath of triumph*) Well—you know that coloured chap she was going to marry? Ahmed Assam, or something. Well—they've just found out that he's *already* married. *And* he's got five children. (*She smirks*)
**Frank** Eh?
**Peggy** Out in the Persian Gulf. A whole *family* he's got. (*Disgusted*) Dirty devil. (*She sniffs*) Lucky she found out in time, isn't it?
**Alison** (*quietly*) Poor Mary.
**Peggy** They got the news this morning it seems, but it was too late to stop the paper coming out. (*To Ethel*) You realize what this means, though, don't you? She can't possibly be the "Bride of the Year" now. They'll have to choose someone else.
**Ethel** Oh, the poor thing. She must be feeling terrible.
**Peggy** Of course, the minute I heard, I rang the *Journal* and had a word with our Edna's Jeremy. Just to see if it *was* true. And of course it was. They're having to look for another girl now—to make the award to—so I should think our Edna stands a better chance than most, wouldn't you? I mean—it's not likely they'll look far with Jeremy on the *doorstep*, so to speak, is it? (*She gives a little laugh*) Well? What do you think?
**Ethel** I don't know, Peggy. I really don't know.
**Peggy** Well, I think it's marvellous news. I can see it all now. Our Edna—"Bride of the Year".
**Frank** I don't see what you're getting all worked up about, Mrs Ramskill. After all, it's only a wedding.
**Peggy** (*chortling*) Only a wedding. Just you wait till *your* turn comes, Frank Edwards. You'll be singing a different tune then.
**Frank** Yes. "Rescue the perishing." You'll not find me getting married for a long time yet.
**Peggy** That's what they all say, but you'll get yourself caught one of these days. (*To Alison*) And that goes for you, too, young Alison.
**Alison** There's not much fear of that.
**Peggy** Oh, I don't know. Get rid of some of that fat, smarten yourself up a bit, and you might strike lucky. You never know.

**Alison** It's not a question of "striking lucky", Mrs Ramskill. And I'm quite happy as I am, at the moment, thank you.
**Peggy** (*kindly*) Rubbish. You'd give your eye teeth to have a young man of your own, and you can't tell me otherwise. It's nothing to be *ashamed* of, love.
**Alison** (*indignantly*) I'm not ashamed. I'm just not interested, that's all.

*Peggy smiles pityingly at Ethel*

And you needn't look like that, Mrs Ramskill. I don't need sympathy from you or anybody else. I'm quite *capable* of finding male companionship if I want it—which I don't—so save your pity for somebody in more need of it, if you don't mind.
**Ethel** (*anxiously*) Alison . . .
**Alison** (*hotly*) If I wanted to throw myself at the first man who came along —like *some* I could mention—I could be married with half-a-dozen children by the time I'd reached thirty.
**Frank** (*trying to lighten the situation*) So long as you didn't throw yourself too hard, and flatten the poor fellow.
**Alison** (*snapping*) You keep out of this, Uncle Frank.
**Peggy** (*uncomfortably*) Well—I'm sorry if I seem to have upset you, Alison. I'm sure I didn't mean . . .
**Alison** Didn't you? Well, that makes a change, doesn't it?
**Ethel** Alison.
**Alison** (*to Ethel*) It's true, isn't it? You *know* it is. Every time she comes round here, she goes on about how fat I am, and what a great pity it is that no man in his right mind would give me a second glance.
**Peggy** (*astonished*) I never . . .
**Alison** (*fighting tears*) Well, I'm sick and tired of it, Mrs Ramskill. I *know* I'm fat and ugly—and short-sighted—and I've got no dress sense, my hair's a mess and I eat too much. I know it, I know it, I *know* it. And I don't need reminding of it every two minutes, thank you very much. (*She bursts into tears*)
**Peggy** (*frostily*) I think I'd better go.
**Frank** Well—you know where the door is, Mrs R. (*He smiles to take away the offence*)
**Ethel** (*going to comfort Alison*) There, there. Don't take on, love.
**Peggy** I'll probably see you some *other* time, Ethel.

*Peggy bites her lip, turns, and exits through the hall*

**Ethel** (*over her shoulder*) All right, Peggy. (*She pats Alison's shoulder*)
**Alison** (*sniffing*) I'm sorry, Mum.
**Ethel** It's all right, love. Don't worry.
**Alison** I shouldn't have said anything.
**Ethel** It's all done with now. Come on. Sit down. (*She leads her to the sofa*)
**Frank** Well—with friends like Peggy around, you certainly don't need enemies, do you?

**Ethel** Oh, she didn't mean any harm, Frank. You know her. She just wasn't thinking. She's too full of bright ideas about Edna winning this "Bride of the Year" award, that's all.

**Frank** It'd serve her right if somebody else won it.

**Ethel** I don't think there's much likelihood of that. Not with Edna being engaged to the Assistant Manager of the paper.

**Frank** Oh. So *that's* the way it is, is it? Nobody else is going to get a look in.

**Alison** (*Wiping her eyes*) I wish somebody else *would* win it. Just for *spite*. It'd wipe that smug look off her face. (*She sniffles*)

**Frank** (*quietly*) Yes. Yes, it would, wouldn't it? (*He thinks*)

**Ethel** (*looking at him sharply*) Frank Edwards. There's something nasty going on in that mind of yours, isn't there? I can see it in your eyes.

**Frank** Mmmmmm. I've just had an idea. (*He moves away slowly*) Somebody *is* going to take that award out of Edna Ramskill's reach.

**Alison** (*looking up slowly*) Who?

**Frank** You. You are.

**Ethel** Are you out of your mind?

**Frank** Not a bit of it. Alison Murchinson. You are going to be the *Journal's* "Bride of the Year"—and get that cash prize to boot.

**Ethel** But Frank . . .

**Frank** (*filled with devilment*) And not only *that*, my chubby little cherub. Just do as I tell you, and you'll have the *Wedding of the Year!* (*He bursts out laughing and dancing about*)

*Alison and Ethel gape at Frank, as—*

*the* CURTAIN *falls*

SCENE 2

*The same. That afternoon*

*The room is neat and tidy once more. Ethel is sitting in the armchair by the fire, talking to Walter who is sitting on the sofa*

**Ethel** . . . Then he burst out laughing, and rushed out of the house as though he'd gone mad.

**Walter** (*scratching his head*) Perhaps he has. And where's he gone to, then?

**Ethel** I've no idea—and it's been three hours now.

**Walter** (*thoughtfully*) Well, he must have something up his sleeve, mustn't he?

**Ethel** I know . . . and that's what's worrying me. He's *always* been one for doing things on impulse. (*Rising*) Oh, I do wish he'd hurry up and come back so I can find out what he's been up to. (*She moves to the window and looks out*)

**Walter** Now stop worrying, woman. He'll know what he's doing.

**Ethel** Maybe—but I know him and his little ideas.

**Walter** I wish I knew our Melvyn's as well as you seem to know your Frank's.

**Ethel** (*turning*) He *is* my step brother.

**Walter** And Melvyn's my son—but wherever he gets his crackpot ideas from I just don't know. They must come from his mother's side, God rest her soul, because they certainly don't come from mine. You know—sometimes I start wondering to myself if the lad's quite sane.

**Ethel** Oh, Walter. He's not as bad as all that.

**Walter** You haven't got to live with him. It's no wonder my hair's going grey. I'm surprised it's not coming out in handfuls.

**Ethel** What's he doing now? Or shouldn't I ask?

**Walter** The last I saw of him, he was working on a new "wonder glue" that's going to revolutionize the market. What the place'll look like when I get back, I shudder to think. In fact—I might never *get* back. He'll most likely have glued all the windows and doors shut. Honestly. Twenty-three years old, and he hasn't the brains he was born with.

**Ethel** Never mind, Walter. Maybe one of these days he'll invent something that *will* work properly, and end up a millionaire. You can always hope. (*She glances out of the window again*)

**Walter** The only thing I hope, is that when he finally decides to blow himself up once and for all—he doesn't take me with him. Any sign of him?

**Ethel** Hmm?

**Walter** Frank. Any sign of him?

**Ethel** (*smiling*) It's not Frank I'm watching for. It's the Aunts. They should have been here ages ago.

**Walter** Perhaps they're not coming?

**Ethel** They'll be coming, all right. The first Saturday in every month. Regular as clockwork.

**Walter** Pity. I thought you might be able to make that drive after all.

**Ethel** Sorry, Walter. But they've never missed. Not once in twenty-four years. They started coming round just after I married Stan, and they've been coming round ever since. Twelve times a year for the last twenty-four.

**Walter** (*surprised*) And *never* missed?

**Ethel** Not once.


*Alison enters from upstairs*


**Alison** (*looking round*) Haven't they arrived *yet*? Aunt Cilla's getting herself into a bit of a state.

**Ethel** (*slightly worried*) No, there's no sign of them. I do hope everything's all right.

**Alison** We'd have heard if it wasn't. It's just that she's a bit on edge—like she always is when they come late.

**Walter** Yes, well I expect it must be a bit worrying, what with them being elderly an' all. But they're bound to turn up shortly.

**Alison** I know. That's what's worrying her. She keeps hoping they'll give it a miss for a change. She says they give her the pip.

**Ethel** (*surprised*) Alison . . .

**Alison** That's what she said. Her very words. The minute they go into her room, she says she turns her deaf-aid off so she won't have to listen to them babbling. If it wasn't for that, she said, she'd go stark, raving bonkers.

**Ethel** Now, Alison. I'm quite sure she didn't say that.

**Alison** Well—it was words to that effect. In any case, she wanted to hear more about Uncle Frank's idea about me being "Bride of the Year".

**Ethel** (*dismayed*) Oh, Alison. Really. You didn't tell her about *that*, did you?

**Alison** (*flopping on to the sofa*) Why not? I thought she could do with a good laugh.

**Walter** You didn't ought to think of it like that, Alison, love. Getting married isn't a joke.

**Alison** It would be if I got married. I suppose it's just possible they could get me to church on a lorry, but could you honestly imagine anybody trying to lift me over the threshold? He'd drop dead of exhaustion, and I'd be left a widow on my wedding day.

**Ethel** (*annoyed*) Don't talk so silly, Alison. You're not *that* big. (*To Walter*) I've never known anybody go on about their size so much as she does, have you? It's an absolute obsession with her. (*To Alison*) There are lots bigger girls than you who get married.

**Walter** Of course there are. Love's got nothing to do with size. It's what a person's like that really matters.

**Alison** That's what I keep telling myself, but none of the men I take a liking to seem to think the same way. They like the tall, willowy blonde types without a brain in their heads. (*Resignedly*) No, I was born fat and I shall die fatter, and that's all there is to it.

**Ethel** (*crossly*) You weren't born fat. You were a perfectly normal and healthy baby.

**Alison** Oh, Mum—I've seen the photographs. I was so fat even then, I bet you didn't have me christened in a font. You probably launched me down a slipway with a bottle of champagne.

**Ethel** (*laughing despite herself*) Really, Alison . . .

*The doorbell chimes*

(*Relieved*) Oh. That'll be the Aunts. Thank goodness for that. Be a love and let them in, Alison.

**Alison** (*rising*) You can slip out the back way if you like, Mr Thornton. I'll keep them talking in the hall.

**Walter** (*puzzled*) Pardon?

**Ethel** Take no notice, Walter. She's in one of those moods again. (*To Alison*) Now go and let them in or they'll think we've gone out. Scoot. (*She begins plumping cushions, etc.*)

**Alison** (*over her shoulder as she goes*) Well, you can't say you weren't warned.

*Alison exits through the hall*

**Walter** (*to Ethel*) I take it she's not overfond? (*He rises*)
**Ethel** (*surprised*) Of the Aunts, you mean? (*She laughs*) Oh, no. She's very fond of them. We all are. They're a bit *odd*, but they're dear old souls, just the same.
**Alison** (*off*) Hello. We'd almost given up hope.
**Honoria** (*off*) Where there's life there's hope.
**Matilda** (*off*) Patience is a virtue.
**Ethel** (*to Walter*) They've arrived.

*Honoria and Matilda Murchinson enter and stand in the arch. They are both in their seventies, and dressed like wax figures from an Edwardian museum. Long coats and dresses, circa 1905, feather boas, and hats topped with enormous nets, dried foliage, stuffed birds and raffia. They both clutch large carpet-bags containing embroidery-rings and silks. They are fussy and inclined to twitter*

**Alison** (*peering over their shoulders*) I'll let Aunt Priscilla know you've arrived.

*Alison exits upstairs*

**Ethel** (*moving to greet them*) Come in, Aunts. Let me have your coats.

*They remove their coats, but retain their hats and the carpet-bags*

Sit down while I hang these up, then I'll make you a nice cup of tea before you go upstairs.

*Ethel goes into the hall with the coats. The Aunts move as one to the sofa and sit, bolt upright, bags perched on their knees*

**Walter** (*smiling*) How do you do?

*Their heads swivel towards him, blankly*

**Ethel** (*returning*) Oh, you'll not have met Walter, will you?

*The Aunts face Ethel*

This is Mr Thornton from next door.

*The Aunts face Walter*

He comes round to do the odd jobs and things when Frank's out.
**Walter** (*nervously*) Always glad to help out, you know.
**Honoria** (*sagely*) A friend in need is a friend indeed.
**Walter** Eh? Oh—yes. Yes, I suppose so.
**Ethel** I'll go and put the kettle on.

*Ethel exits to the kitchen*

*The Aunts gaze silently at Walter*

**Walter** (*a little uncomfortable*) Yes. Well . . . it's like I always say. You never know when you might need a bit of help yourself, do you?
**Matilda** Great oaks from little acorns grow.
**Walter** Sorry?
**Honoria** One good turn deserves another.
**Walter** Oh. Yes—yes. (*He sits in the easy chair*) Yes.

*There is deathly silence. Walter and the Aunts stare at each other. As if on a signal, the two ladies dive their hands into their bags and produce embroidery rings, silks and needles, then begin to stitch furiously*

You—er—you like to keep busy, I see?
**Matilda** The devil finds work for idle hands.
**Walter** Er—yes. I suppose he does. (*He coughs*) For yourselves, are they? Or do you do them for charities?
**Honoria** Charity begins at home.
**Walter** Oh. (*He lapses into silence as they stitch on*)

*Ethel enters from the kitchen with a tray holding four cups, saucers, side plates, and tea things. She crosses to the coffee-table and puts the tray on it*

**Ethel** Won't be long. (*She smiles*)
**Walter** (*rising eagerly*) Is there anything I can do to help?
**Ethel** No thank you, Walter. You sit and talk to the Aunts. This is Aunt Honoria, and this is Aunt Matilda.
**Walter** (*desperately*) I don't mind helping.
**Matilda** Too many cooks spoil the broth.
**Walter** Yes—but many hands make light work.

*The Aunts stop stitching with shock and look up. They look at Walter, then at each other, then their heads go down again and they resume stitching*

**Ethel** (*crossing back to the kitchen*) But there's nothing to do, Walter. Honestly. I'm only waiting for the kettle to boil. You sit yourself down and relax.

*Ethel exits to the kitchen*

*Walter sits again and gazes at the Aunts. They carry on working, then suddenly look up, lock eyes with him, look at each other, nod in unison, then their heads go down again and they resume work*

**Walter** (*clearing his throat*) You—er—you don't see many women doing embroidery these days, do you? (*No reaction*) Not like they used to do. (*No reaction*) They don't seem to have the patience for it, do they?

*Matilda looks up and opens her mouth to speak. Honoria nudges her and shakes her head. Matilda's mouth closes again*

I hear it can take years to do one of them big ones. Must seem never-ending, mustn't it?

*Matilda looks at Honoria, who nods. Matilda smiles*

**Matilda** It's a long road that has no turning.
**Walter** Aye. (*He slumps back in the chair*)

*The Aunts resume their needlework and silence reigns. Desperately Walter tries again*

Nice day, isn't it? (*Silence*) Makes a change after all that rain we've had lately. (*Silence*) If it carries on like this we'll all be ending up with a suntan, won't we?
**Honoria** One swallow doesn't make a summer.
**Walter** (*beaten*) No.

*Alison enters from upstairs*

**Alison** (*to the Aunts*) I've told Aunt Priscilla you've arrived. She says you needn't hurry up if you'd like a long tea. (*She goes to the window and looks out*) Mum in the kitchen?
**Walter** Yes.
**Alison** I suppose I'd better go and see if she needs a hand.
**Walter** (*quickly*) No. I mean—she doesn't. I've asked her—but she said no.
**Alison** (*grinning at him and indicating the Aunts from behind*) Too many cooks?
**Walter** (*nodding*) Aye. That's right.
**Alison** (*smiling wickedly*) Looks like the weather's changing again. There's a big black cloud heading this way. (*She points at the back of Honoria*)
**Honoria** (*without looking up*) Behind every cloud there's a silver lining.
**Alison** I wish it would go away. (*She points at Matilda's back*)
**Matilda** (*stitching on*) If wishes were horses, beggars would ride.

*Alison and Walter snigger silently*

**Alison** (*mouthing to Walter*) Now you try.
**Walter** (*mouthing*) Me? (*He thinks*) Er—I've never *seen* a cloud as black as that before, have you?
**Matilda** }
**Honoria** } It's always darkest before the dawn. { (*Speaking together*)

*Alison and Walter dissolve into silent laughter*

*Ethel enters with the teapot*

**Ethel** (*going to the coffee-table*) What's so funny?

**Alison** (*trying to keep a straight face*) Nothing. We were just having a little laugh, that's all.

**Matilda** He who laughs last . . .

**Honoria** Laughs best.

*Walter and Alison look at each other and once more dissolve into silent giggles. Ethel pours tea*

**Ethel** (*to the Aunts*) Do you want to take your tea up with you? Or would you rather stay down here?

**Matilda** (*archly*) A nod's as good as a wink to a blind man. (*She rises*)

**Ethel** (*blankly*) Pardon?

**Honoria** (*rising*) There's none so blind as those who *won't* see.

*The Aunts pick up their tea and belongings and move to the arch*

**Ethel** (*bewildered*) I'm sorry—but you've lost me.

**Matilda** (*glancing at Walter, roguishly*) Look before you leap. (*She titters*)

**Ethel** (*realizing*) Oh—no. No. You've got it all wrong. We're not . . .

**Honoria** (*wagging her finger*) Least said—soonest mended. (*She beams*)

*The Aunts give a last glance at Walter, giggle, then totter out into the hall, exiting up the stairs*

**Walter** What was all that about?

**Ethel** (*embarrassed*) They think we're—well—you know. A bit more than friends. (*She pours tea to hide her confusion*)

**Walter** (*surprised*) Eh?

**Alison** (*laughing*) If you could only have seen your face, Mr Thornton, when I came in. You looked *petrified*.

**Walter** I felt it as well. I didn't know what to *say* to them. Are they always like that?

**Alison** Always.

**Ethel** (*handing a cup to Walter*) I'm sorry, Walter. I shouldn't have left you alone with them without giving you warning. I keep forgetting you're not used to them like us.

**Walter** (*taking the cup*) Never mind. It's an ill wind that blows no good. There . . . now they've got me at it as well.

*They all laugh. The doorbell chimes*

**Alison** I'll go.

*Alison exits to the hall*

**Ethel** Cake, Walter?

**Walter** Just a small piece.

**Melvyn** (*off*) Oh—hello, Alison. Sorry to trouble you, but is my dad here?

*Walter looks up*

**Alison** (*off*) Yes, come in, Melvyn. They're in the living-room. (*Sharply*) Mind that stand. (*Louder*) Melvyn . . .!

*There is a great crash from the hall*

**Walter** (*jumping up*) Melvyn!

*Ethel hurries to the arch*

**Ethel** (*distressed as she looks off*) Oh—Melvyn.

*Melvyn Thornton enters, looking dishevelled. He is an untidy-looking young man in his twenties, and splattered with paint, etc. He clutches a large paintbrush which is caked with a reddish-brown gunge*

**Alison** (*off*) It's all right, Mum. It's just the paintwork and a couple of broken pegs.

*Ethel looks reproachfully at Melvyn, who hangs his head*

**Melvyn** (*uneasily*) I'm sorry, Mrs Murchinson. I just didn't notice it.
**Walter** (*glowering*) What do you mean, didn't notice it? It's been standing there for two years to my knowledge.
**Melvyn** I forgot.
**Walter** (*spluttering*) Forgot? Forgot? How can you forget something the size of a hallstand?
**Ethel** (*smiling bravely*) Never mind, Melvyn. Accidents will happen.
**Walter** (*snorting*) You're telling me. And with him around, I don't need reminding of it. (*To Melvyn*) What do you want?
**Melvyn** Well—I just came round to tell you the good news.
**Walter** You're leaving home?
**Melvyn** No. (*He laughs nervously*) The good news about my glue. You know—the glue I've been working on. Down in the shed.
**Walter** Aye.
**Melvyn** (*happily*) It works.

*Alison enters from the hall, wiping her hands*

It really does. I've tried it. It'll stick wood, tin, plastic, paper, glass, brick, porcelain—anything. I'm going to——
**Walter** (*interrupting*) Hold on a minute. Hold on. What did you say just then?
**Melvyn** (*uncertainly*) Just when?
**Walter** Just then. When you said it'd stick porcelain.
**Melvyn** Oh. That. (*Quickly*) Yes, well it *does*. You've only got to touch something with it and it's stuck for good. It'll never come off. (*To Ethel*) They'll be able to use it on aircr——
**Walter** (*interrupting again*) How do you *know* that it sticks porcelain, Melvyn?
**Melvyn** (*uneasily*) Well—because I've tried it. (*To Ethel*) So if there's anything you want sticking before——

**Walter** (*interrupting again*) Melvyn!

*Melvyn stops*

Did you say you'd *tried* it?

*Melvyn nods uneasily*

On porcelain?

*Melvyn nods again*

And whence came the porcelain—or shouldn't I *ask*?

*Melvyn gulps and turns to Ethel*

**Melvyn** I'll mend that hallstand for you now, Mrs Murchinson . . .
**Walter** Melvyn!
**Melvyn** (*even more quickly*) It won't take me a minute. I'll just go and get
the——
**Walter** (*interrupting, in a bellow*) MELVYN!

*Everyone jumps. Melvyn turns round, fearfully*

I asked you a question. Where did the porcelain come from?
**Melvyn** (*gulping*) Off the floor.
**Walter** (*menacing*) And what was it *doing* on the floor, Melvyn?
**Ethel** Oh, really, Walter. How would *he* know? Somebody probably just
dropped it there.
**Walter** Yes. And that's just what I'm afraid of—isn't it, Melvyn?
**Melvyn** (*backing away*) It was an accident.
**Walter** I'll bet it was. And there's going to be *another* one in a minute.
Come here. (*He advances on Melvyn*)
**Ethel** Walter. What *is* it? What's he done?
**Walter** (*grimly*) I'll tell you what he's done, Ethel. He's smashed a three-
hundred-year-old Chinese porcelain vase that his Uncle Arnold in
Australia gave me as a wedding present. *That's* what he's done.
**Ethel** (*gazing at Melvyn in horror*) Oh, Melvyn.
**Melvyn** It was an accident, Dad. Honest it was. But it's all right now.
I've glued it back together again with my new glue. (*He waves the brush*)
It's set like concrete and you can't even see the cracks.
**Walter** I hope for your sake that you can't. Where is it? I'd best take a
look.
**Melvyn** It—er—it's on the front room table. (*He gulps*) Stuck.
**Walter** Stuck???
**Melvyn** (*quickly*) Well, I had to put it somewhere to glue it together again,
didn't I? And I must have let a drop of glue get on the base without
noticing. By the time I'd finished, it'd set solid and I couldn't move it.

*Alison smothers a laugh and Ethel glances at her*

**Walter** (*aghast*) Do you mean to tell me we've got a three-hundred-year-
old, four foot high Chinese porcelain vase stuck in the middle of the
table? For keeps?

**Melvyn** Of course we haven't. It's at the edge. I wouldn't have been able to reach it in the middle.

*Alison rocks with laughter*

**Walter** (*almost purple with rage*) You great, stupid, idiotic, useless lump of . . . And what are we supposed to do when we want to use it? How do we get a cloth on to it?
**Melvyn** (*helpfully*) Cut a hole in it?

*Alison shrieks*

**Walter** (*fuming*) I'll kill him. I'll *kill* him
**Ethel** (*laughing*) Now calm down, Walter. Loosing your temper isn't going to help matters, is it? Perhaps he'll be able to do something about it.
**Walter** Like what, for instance?
**Ethel** Well—like inventing something to *soften* the glue again.
**Walter** (*fuming*) I'll soften him.
**Ethel** Come on, Walter. Where's your sense of humour? (*To Melvyn*) Wipe that worried look off your face, Melvyn, and sit down for a minute. I'll get you a cup of tea.
**Melvyn** (*relieved*) Oh—thank you. (*He puts the brush down on one of the chairs beside the arch*)
**Walter** (*yelling*) Melvyn . . .!

*Melvyn jumps and spins to face Walter*

The brush!

*Realization dawns, and Melvyn leaps for the brush handle. He gives a heave and the seat of the chair rips away from its new cover, firmly fixed to the brush*

**Melvyn** (*gaping at it in horror*) Oh, heck.
**Ethel** (*petrified*) My new chair cover.

*Walter covers his eyes*

**Alison** (*shrieking with laughter again*) Oh, Melvyn. (*She holds her sides*) I can't stand it.
**Melvyn** (*miserably*) I'm ever so sorry, Mrs Murchinson. (*He plucks at the cover*)
**Ethel** (*brokenly*) So am I.
**Melvyn** It won't come off. (*He looks round helplessly*)
**Walter** If the Germans had only had him during the last war—we'd have surrendered. (*Tiredly*) Oh, Ethel, I'm sorry. I wouldn't have had this happen for the world.
**Ethel** I've only just had them done, as well.
**Walter** I'll see they get repaired properly for you, Ethel, and useless there can pay for them.
**Ethel** (*with a sigh*) Oh, it doesn't matter. Really it doesn't. Sit down, Melvyn. I'll get you that tea. (*She turns back to the table*)
**Melvyn** Would you like me to give you a hand? (*He moves forward*)

**Ethel** (*almost in a shriek*) No! (*Recovering herself*) I mean—no, thank you. It's all ready. Just you—sit down.

**Walter** (*glaring at him*) Yes. You've done enough damage for one day.

*Melvyn sits timidly on the sofa and Ethel pours him a cup of tea. He smiles weakly as she hands it to him*

**Melvyn** Thank you. (*He looks round helplessly for somewhere to put the brush*)

**Ethel** I'll take that, shall I? (*She takes the brush*) I'll try soaking it in the bathroom sink. Perhaps that'll loosen it.

*Ethel exits through the arch, throwing a rueful look at the ruined seat as she goes*

*Walter and Melvyn look at each other. Walter scowls and Melvyn looks quickly away to watch Alison, who is just about recovering. He smiles weakly*

**Melvyn** Nice day, isn't it?

*Alison bursts out laughing again. Melvyn looks blank*

*Frank enters from the hall with Harry Elphinstone. Harry is about thirty-three, very "with it" in dress and sporting a pair of owl-like spectacles. He looks very much the English equivalent of Yves St Laurent*

**Frank** I'm back. (*He indicates Alison to Harry*) Well—there she is.

**Harry** (*studying her*) Hmmmm. Yes. I see what you mean. (*He moves around her*) Yes—yes.

**Alison** (*amused*) Hey—what is this?

**Frank** This—my dear little niece—is the great Harry Elphinstone himself. Dress-designer extraordinaire—Britains greatest young fashion expert—and creator-to-be of your wedding gown. All the way from Oxfordshire.

**Alison** (*gaping*) Oh. (*Dazed*) How do you do?

**Melvyn** Wedding gown? (*To Alison*) I didn't know you were getting married, Alison.

**Alison** (*recovering*) I'm not. This is just one of Uncle Frank's mad ideas, that's all. (*She begins to move away*)

**Harry** (*still observing her thoughtfully*) Ahhhh—don't move.

*Alison stops dead in her tracks*

**Frank** (*to Alison*) Not getting married indeed. Ficklety, they call you women.

**Alison** *Frailty*, thy name is woman, if you must quote—and there's nothing frail about me.

**Frank** Of course there isn't, my sweet one. That's why I've brought Harry chasing across the country. He can make an airship look like a vision of loveliness.

**Alison** Well, thank *you*.

**Frank** Harry. This is Mr Thornton from next door, and Melvyn, his only pride and joy.

**Walter** Thank goodness.

**Melvyn** Hello. (*He puts his hand out to Harry forgetting he still has his cup in it*) Oh—sorry. (*He puts the cup down on the table and extends his hand once more—still holding the cup*) Oh, heck. (*He tugs at the cup*) It's stuck to me. I must have got some of the glue on my fingers. (*He looks up, panic-stricken*)

**Alison** (*gurgling*) Oh, no. Not again.

**Harry** What's wrong?

**Walter** It's this flaming glue he's just concocted. It's stuck him to the cup. (*He rises*)

**Frank** (*uncomprehendingly*) Done what? Stuck him—here. (*He gets hold of the cup and pulls*) Hey . . .

**Melvyn** (*anxiously*) Mind your fingers.

**Frank** (*tugging*) Pull.

**Melvyn** I am doing. It won't come off.

*Frank heaves*

Owww!

**Alison** (*chortling*) Looks like it's stuck there for good, Melvyn.

*Frank tugs again*

**Melvyn** Owwwwwww!

**Harry** Watch the tea. It's slopping over.

**Frank** Heave! (*He tugs*)

**Melvyn** Owwwwwwwwwww! (*He staggers to his feet*)

**Walter** Watch the carpet! You'll have it all over.

**Frank** Hold it. Hold it. Look—*we'll* pull the cup, and you two hang on to Melvyn. That should do it.

*With much giggling, Alison gets behind Melvyn and hooks her fingers into his waistband. Walter holds on to her. Frank and Harry grasp the cup*

**Frank** Ready? Pulllllll!

*They all heave and Melvyn yells*

**Melvyn** You're stretching my aaaaaaaaaaaarm!

*Alison, still giggling madly, suddenly shoots backwards as Melvyn's trouser seat comes away in her hand to reveal his underpants. She cannons into Walter and they fall on to the sofa. Melvyn, Frank and Harry shoot forward, but manage to retain their balance. Melvyn lets go of the cup to cover his rear end*

**Frank** (*triumphantly*) It's off.

**Melvyn** So are my trousers. (*He attempts to hide the hole*)

**Walter** (*struggling up*) It could only happen to Melvyn.

**Alison** (*getting up, and still laughing*) Never mind, Mr Thornton. It's off now.

**Frank** That's all very well—but what do *I* do? (*He holds up the cup*)

*Everyone reacts*

Only joking. (*He laughs*) Hmmm. (*He examines the cup*) Not even sticky.

**Melvyn** (*surprised*) Eh?

**Harry** (*looking*) Dry as a bone.

**Melvyn** But it can't be. (*He edges over to look*) What about my glue? (*He takes the cup and looks at it, mystified*) It's gone. Vanished.

**Walter** And a good job it has, otherwise you'd have been walking around for the rest of your life with that thing stuck to you.

**Alison** And that really *would* upset Mum. It's one of a set.

**Melvyn** (*puzzled*) I can't understand it. (*He peers into the cup*) Oh, hey— look. It's crystallized. It must have been the heat from the tea that caused it. Isn't that fantastic?

**Walter** Amazing. And I'll be even more amazed when you get that vase off the front room table, so bring your body. We're going home. If you stay here much longer, they'll have no home left to live in.

**Melvyn** But Dad . . .

**Walter** Never mind "But Dad". Move! (*To Alison*) Thank your mother for the tea, love, and tell her I'll see her later about the damage. (*He moves up to the arch*)

**Melvyn** (*sidling after him*) 'Bye, Alison—Frank—Mr Elphinton.

**Harry** Stone. Elphinstone.

**Melvyn** Oh, yes. Elphin—er—stone.

*Walter grabs his shoulder and propels him out at great speed*

*Alison collapses on to the sofa, bubbling with laughter. Harry stares after Walter and Melvyn. Frank moves to the easy chair*

**Harry** Was that for real?

**Alison** 'Fraid so.

**Harry** I don't believe it. (*He shakes his head*)

**Frank** (*leaning on the chair back*) It's true all right. Melvyn the Mad, that's him. A living example of an accident looking for somewhere to happen. Anyway, sit down, Elf, old son, and give with the details.

**Alison** What details?

*Harry sits beside Alison*

**Frank** The details of your wedding dress, dopey.

**Alison** (*sobering*) Oh, give it a rest, Uncle. The joke's over.

**Frank** What joke?

**Alison** *You* know. About me being elected "Bride of the Year". It's not funny any more.

**Frank** It's not supposed to be funny. I'm deadly serious. That's why I've been dashing all over town like someone demented, and Harry's come over to have a look at you. He's going to make the dress for you, aren't you, Elph? Well, don't just sit there. Tell the girl.

**Harry** (*with a nervous cough*) That's right—Miss—er—Alison.

**Alison** Now I *know* I'm dreaming. *You* designing a dress for *me*? We couldn't even begin to afford you. You're too . . .

**Harry** Expensive? Not to an old bodyguard like Frank. I owe *him* a few favours. Saved me from many a beating-up in the past, he did.

**Alison** When?

**Harry** At school, of course. My life used to be hell till Frank came along. He soon sorted them out for me.

**Alison** Who? Bullies?

**Harry** (*nodding*) I was a natural target for them. Undersized, timid, shy. Face half-hidden with horn-rims, and the most awful lisp you've ever heard in your life. I used to get bashed at least twice a week until I met Frank.

**Frank** Yes—well I'm sure she must be absolutely fascinated by your life story and my valiant deeds of yesteryear, but you came over to talk to her about a wedding dress, remember?

**Alison** Now just a minute—the pair of you. (*To Frank*) I want you to drop whatever mad scheme you're churning around in that tiny Chinese mind of yours, and leave me alone. Understand?

**Frank** I thought you wanted to get married?

**Alison** I do. But not just yet.

**Frank** (*to Harry*) Now she tells me. It's only this morning she was crying her eyes out——

**Alison** Uncle . . .

**Frank** (*continuing*) —because some stuck-up snob told her that she'd never be able to get herself a husband because she was fat as a bacon pig, and no man would look at her twice . . .

**Alison** Uncle.

**Frank** At that moment, she was ready to commit *murder* to prove that she could get a man of her own—and look at her now. Only three hours later and it's all forgotten.

**Alison** That was different. I was upset then.

**Frank** I know you were. You're upset every time somebody tells you the same thing. Have been for years. Yet the first time you get a chance to show them all they're wrong, you chicken out.

**Alison** (*hotly*) I'm not chickening out. It's just that the whole thing is so stupid. How can somebody like me be elected "Bride of the Year"? It's ridiculous. I'm so fat that the vicar would have to do the ceremony twice to make sure he'd covered both ends of me.

**Harry** If you don't mind me butting in on a family argument, Miss Murchinson, you're talking out of the back of your head. I'm not saying I *agree* with what Frank has in mind, but I must put you straight on one thing. You're not fat. You're just well built.

**Alison** Yes. I'm as well built as the Great Wall of China—and not far off the same width.

**Frank** I shall shake you, in a minute.

**Alison** (*firmly*) Uncle Frank. I'm twenty-three years old—nearly twenty-four—and I know what I am. I'm fat, plain and unattractive to the opposite sex, and there's nothing that anybody can do about it. I've never even had a *boy* friend of my own.

**Frank** And whose fault is that? You hide yourself away in the house here, stuffing yourself with cream cakes and chocolates, dressing like a refugee from Oxfam, and hardly ever going out. How do you expect to meet anybody?

**Alison** I go to work.

**Frank** Yes—in a telephone exchange where nobody can see you. Good grief, child. You'll never get yourself married at this rate.

**Alison** (*stung*) All right, Grandad. So I'll never get married. Why should that worry *you*?

**Frank** Because I want to see you happy, Alison. That's why.

**Alison** I *am* happy.

**Frank** No you're not. You're as miserable as sin.

**Alison** And not half so attractive.

**Frank** (*groaning*) Look. There's nothing *wrong* with your looks.

**Alison** Apart from my squinty eyes.

**Frank** You've not got squinty eyes. You're short-sighted, that's all. That's nothing a pair of contact lenses couldn't fix. And while we're on the subject of looks, a bit of make-up now and then wouldn't do you any harm.

**Alison** What do you recommend? Polyfilla?

**Frank** I give up. You talk to her, Elph. (*He sits in the easy chair*)

**Harry** Look, Miss Murchinson—Alison. It seems to me you've got some sort of complex about yourself. One that's quite unfounded. There's nothing wrong with your looks, and you're not as—as . . .

**Alison** Fat?

**Harry** All right. Fat. You're not half as fat as you think you are.

*Alison's brows rise*

I don't suppose you'll believe any of what I'm saying, but I promise you—just leave everything to me, and I'll guarantee you'll cause a sensation when you walk down that aisle.

**Alison** (*drily*) It wouldn't surprise me. I'll be walking down it on my own. I don't even have a fiancé.

**Frank** I'll get round to that later. Let's get the important things out of the way first. Show her the design, Elphie. See what she has to say about *that*.

**Alison** Design?

**Harry** (*producing a folded sheet of paper from his coat*) I took the liberty of knocking up a rough sketch before coming over. (*He hands it to her*) Naturally it's not the finished thing, but at least you can see the idea I had in mind.

*Alison opens the paper and looks. Harry and Frank watch her anxiously*

**Frank** Well? Do you like it?

*There is utter silence. Frank looks at Harry, who looks back at him. Alison continues to look at the sketch*

**Harry** If you don't like it, you've only got to say so. I can always do you another to your own specifications.

**Alison** (*softly*) Oh, no. It's beautiful. It really is.

**Frank** (*relieved and pleased*) You see? What did I tell you? Can't you see yourself in it? How sensational you're going to look? Now who's got mad schemes, eh?

*Alison bursts into tears, drops the paper, and hurries off into the parlour, sobbing her heart out*

**Harry** (*to Frank*) Hadn't you better . . .?

**Frank** No. She'll be all right. Just give her a few minutes to get over it, and she'll be back. (*He rises*) Well? What do you think, then?

**Harry** (*picking up the sketch and putting it away*) You want the truth?

**Frank** Natch.

**Harry** I think she's a mess—in her mind, of course. She's managed to convince herself that she's plain and unattractive, and that there's nothing anybody can do about it.

**Frank** And?

**Harry** She's wrong. Absolutely wrong. There's nothing wrong with her figure that a good diet wouldn't cure, and a few hours in a beauty parlour would work wonders with her complexion. All she needs is the incentive.

**Frank** So we give it to her. Once she's won this award, she'll never look back.

**Harry** Maybe.

*Frank looks puzzled*

Have you ever thought what might happen if she *doesn't* win it?

**Frank** I don't follow you.

**Harry** If she doesn't win it, she's going to be more convinced than ever that she's unattractive. And then what?

**Frank** (*laughing*) You don't have to worry about that, Elphie. She can't fail to win. Not in that gown of yours.

**Harry** (*seriously*) Look—I hate to disillusion you, Frank, but a thing like this isn't won by a wedding gown—even if it is one of mine. There are dozens of things to be taken into consideration. Who the guests are. Where the honeymoon will be. Who the family are. Et cetera, et cetera.

**Frank** It's all arranged. Guest list headed by His Worship the Mayor, whose darling little daughter I happen to be seeing rather a lot of these days—*and* who'll be one of the bridesmaids. Honeymoon in the Canary Islands—provided by Freddie Andrews at the Travel Agency at reduced rates, and the family speaks for itself, doesn't it? Aunt Cilla is one of the richest women in the district, and young Alison happens to be her favourite niece.

**Harry** (*patiently*) But what about the most important item of the lot? The groom?

**Frank** Yes—well—that is a bit of a problem, I must admit, but I'll sort something out. We can always cross that bridge when we get to it.

**Harry** I hate to say this, Frank, but you've not only come to it, you're half way across. You booked the photographer an hour ago *and* the reception hall.

**Frank** Well, there's no point in wasting time, is there? We want everything cut and dried in plenty of time. There's going to be no slip-ups at *this* wedding.

**Harry** *What* wedding? You've not even got her to agree to it yet. I think you're making a big mistake, Frank. A very big mistake.

**Frank** Rubbish.

**Harry** But she's got no-one to marry.

*Ethel enters from upstairs, with crockery*

**Ethel** Who hasn't?

**Frank** Oh, hi, Sis. We were just talking about Alison. Oh, this is Harry Elphinstone the designer. My sister Ethel.

**Ethel** *(flustered)* Oh . . .

**Harry** How do you do?

**Ethel** Oh, you must excuse me. I'm a bit overloaded at the moment. I— er—I'll put the kettle on. Won't be a minute. *(She moves to the kitchen)* What was that about Alison, Frank?

**Frank** I was just saying that I've got everything fixed but the groom.

**Ethel** *(curiously)* Fixed up for what?

**Frank** Alison's wedding.

**Ethel** Oh—that.

*Ethel exits to the kitchen*

**Harry** *(to Frank)* She knows about this? What you're doing?

**Frank** Of course she knows. What do you think I am?

*There is a loud crash of crockery from the kitchen. They look at each other*

*Ethel hurries in*

**Ethel** Alison's *what*?

**Frank** Wedding.

**Ethel** But she isn't even *engaged*, yet.

**Frank** So?

**Ethel** You just said you'd got everything fixed up.

**Frank** *(cheerfully)* That's right. Eleven-thirty. Saturday morning. Six weeks from today.

**Ethel** *(weakly)* Six weeks? *(She collapses into the easy chair)* You must be out of your *mind*.

**Frank** Well, if that's all the thanks I'm going to get . . .

**Ethel** *(fuming)* What have you done? What arrangements have you made? Come on. Out with it. I want to know now before it's too late.

**Frank** Don't get excited . . .

**Ethel** (*rising*) Excited? I'm blazing *mad*. What do you mean—running around the town making arrangements for a non-existent wedding? Just who do you think you are?

**Frank** Here—hold on a minute . . .

**Ethel** (*loudly*) Frank Edwards, you haven't got the brains you were born with.

**Frank** Ethel . . .

**Ethel** I'd have thought that you, of all people, would have had more sense than to do something as stupid and irresponsible as what you've just done. Heaven knows what that poor girl's going to feel like if she ever finds out about it. She's upset enough as it is.

**Frank** But she does know. That's what Elph's here for. He's making the dress for her.

**Ethel** He's making nothing for her. (*To Harry*) I'm sorry you've been troubled by this madman, Mr Elphinstone, but I'm afraid we won't be needing your services after all.

**Frank** But Ethel . . .

**Ethel** No.

**Frank** I thought you *wanted* her to be the "Bride of the Year".

**Ethel** Of course I do. Wouldn't any mother? But when she decides to get married, she'll do it in her own good time, and not be given away as first prize in a raffle. Understand? She's not a lump of meat in a cattle market. She's a human being and she's got feelings like everybody else. And just as a matter of interest, Frank Edwards, when she does make up her mind to marry, she'll be the "Bride of the Year" to *me*, whoever the newspapers happen to choose, so there.

**Frank** (*defeated*) All right. All right. We'll call the whole thing off.

**Ethel** *You'll* call the whole thing off. It was your idea.

**Frank** Yes. All right. You needn't go on any more. I'm sorry.

**Ethel** I should think so, too. (*She looks round*) Where is she?

**Harry** (*indicating the parlour*) She went in there.

**Ethel** I'd better go see her. (*She moves to the parlour door*)

**Frank** Come on, Elph. We'd better start cancelling things.

*Alison enters*

**Alison** Uncle Frank. (*She dabs at her eyes*)

**Ethel** Alison, love. (*She puts her arm around her shoulders*)

**Alison** I'm all right, Mum. Really I am. (*She sniffles*)

**Ethel** I've just heard what he's done, the great stupid oaf, but don't worry. We'll soon have everything put right again. He's just on his way to cancel all the arrangements he's been making so busily.

**Alison** (*quickly*) Oh, no. I don't want them cancelling, Mum. I want to go through with it.

*Everyone looks stunned*

**Ethel** Alison—you *can't*.

**Alison** Why not? Take a look at me. A good, hard look. I'm not the world's best catch, am I? I'm plain and I'm fat, and nobody in their right mind is going to look at me twice. I stand about as much chance of getting married by my own efforts as the North Pole does of catching fire.

**Ethel** Alison, love. What's so important about getting married? It's not the be all and end all of life.

**Alison** Maybe not, but if Uncle Frank can find somebody willing to marry me—and take me for what I am—then I'll accept him. No questions asked.

**Ethel** (*horrified*) You don't know what you're saying.

**Alison** Yes I do, Mum. People get married in several countries who've never even seen each other before, and they seem to work out all right. The families arrange everything.

**Ethel** But Alison . . .

**Alison** Sorry, Mum. The only thing I ask is that he's young and clean. (*To Frank*) It's up to you now, Uncle Frank.

**Frank** Now just a minute, Alison. Are you *quite* sure about this? I mean— I don't want you to——

**Alison** (*interrupting*) Quite sure.

*Ethel flops into the easy chair*

There'll be no recriminations, I promise you. (*To Harry*) And I'd like to say that I think your design for the dress is the most beautiful thing I've ever seen in my life. I shall be very proud to wear it.

**Harry** (*slowly*) Thank you.

**Frank** (*brightening*) So it's all on again. Well, all we've got to do now is find a bridegroom and book the church.

**Ethel** If you do, Frank Edwards, I'll never speak to you again so long as I live. Do you hear me?

**Alison** And if you try to stop him, Mum, I'll never speak to *you*. This is the best chance I've ever had in my life, and I'm going to take hold of it with both hands.

**Frank** That's my girl. (*To Ethel*) Don't worry, Sis. I promise you I'll find her the perfect match. You wouldn't be able to choose a better man for her yourself. Honest.

**Ethel** (*bitterly*) I wouldn't have the nerve to try.

**Frank** He'll be tall, dark, and—reasonably handsome. Have a sense of humour, charm and he won't be short of ready cash. (*He thinks hard*) Now who do I know would fit the bill?

*Melvyn appears in the arch*

**Melvyn** Sorry to bother you again, but I've come for my brush. Have you got it?

*Frank turns slowly and looks at Melvyn*

**Frank** (*with a gleam in his eye*) Melvyn.

**Alison** (*spotting it*)  Melvyn?? (*She looks at him with dismay*)
**Ethel** (*rising*)  Melvyn???
**Melvyn** (*startled*)  Is something wrong?
**Frank** (*flinging his arm around Melvyn*)  Not a thing, old son. Not a thing.
  In fact I'd go so far as to say that everything in the garden is *lovely*.

*Various emotions register on everyone's faces as—*

                    *the* CURTAIN *falls*

# ACT II

## SCENE 1

*The same. Saturday evening*

*Once again the room is neat and tidy, except for the damaged chair by the arch. The curtains are drawn and the fire glows brightly. The lights are on but the room is empty. After a moment, voices are heard off, and Frank enters from upstairs, followed by Alison. He wears only a pair of slacks and his socks, and Alison is still in the clothes she wore in the previous act. She carries Frank's shoes*

**Alison** (*as they enter*) Uncle Frank. Listen to me for a minute, will you?

**Frank** (*looking around, harassed*) There isn't time. He'll be here in a minute. Where the devil's my shirt got to? The one with the turn-back cuffs? Why is it you can never *find* anything in this house? (*He calls into the parlour*) Sis!

**Alison** It's being washed. You wore it on Thursday night.

**Frank** (*calling again*) Sis? (*To Alison*) Where is she?

**Alison** I don't know. She *was* upstairs. (*She holds out the shoes*) Here are your shoes, anyway.

**Frank** (*taking them*) They're a fat lot of good if I haven't got a shirt to wear. I can't go down to the pub looking like Tarzan. They'll think I've gone crackers. (*He calls again, louder*) Sis!

**Alison** But you've got dozens of shirts in the wardrobe. And what's wrong with the one in there? (*She indicates the parlour*)

**Frank** Oh, all right. It'll have to do. Be an angel and get it for me, will you? (*He sits on the sofa*)

**Alison** Not till you sit still for a minute and listen to what I want to tell you.

**Frank** (*putting his shoes on*) I *know* what you want to tell me. You want to tell me the same thing you've been telling me since Melvyn Thornton walked out of this room this afternoon. Right?

**Alison** Right. Now all I'm going to say——

**Frank** (*interrupting*) Is nothing. You said this afternoon—in front of witnesses—that you would marry *anyone* I chose for you—providing he was clean and young. True or not true?

**Alison** Well, yes—but I didn't think you were going to——

**Frank** (*interrupting*) Never mind what you *didn't* think. You said *anybody*. And I've found somebody, haven't I? (*He peers at the shoes*) Have you polished these?

**Alison** (*protesting*) But Melvyn *Thornton* . . .

**Frank** (*slipping the shoe on*) What's wrong with him? Apart from the obvious, of course. He's young, clean, and not bad looking—if you keep your eyes half closed—and besides—he'll be out at work for most of the day in any case. The chap's ideal.

**Alison** But I don't love him.

**Frank** Since when did that become one of the qualifications? Look—you don't have to love him. Just get used to him. Now get me that shirt, will you?

**Alison** (*firmly*) I'm not marrying Melvyn Thornton.

**Frank** Why not? Go on. Tell me.

**Alison** (*helplessly*) Because he's *Melvyn*. That's why not.

*Frank looks at her steadily*

Oh—(*miserably*)—it's not only that, Uncle Frank. I *like* him well enough. He's sweet and kind and—and . . . (*She is lost for words*) It's just that he's so *peculiar*.

**Frank** Peculiar?

**Alison** Well—the way everything he does goes wrong. Like the folding-ladder that folded when he was halfway up it, and the electric fan that shot through the kitchen window because it was too powerful. Those self-lighting cigarettes that nearly burned Mr Thornton alive when they all went off at once, and the glue this afternoon. Nothing goes right for him.

**Frank** And that's the reason you don't want to marry him, is it? Because nothing goes right for him.

**Alison** (*stung*) Well, would *you* marry him?

**Frank** People might talk if I did.

**Alison** Oh, don't *joke* about it. I'm serious. I know I said I'd marry any-body—but I never expected you to pick on Melvyn.

**Frank** But I did, didn't I? And I've asked him to come round and have a drink with me tonight, haven't I? That's why I'm racing around like somebody not right in the head, trying to get ready for him. Now you turn round and calmly inform me that you've got no intention of going through with it. Well, all right then. As soon as he arrives, I'll tell him that we're not going out for that drink after all. Does that suit you?

**Alison** There's nothing to stop you going out for a drink, is there? You can still do that.

**Frank** What's the point? The only reason I asked him out was to set the plan in motion and get him to propose to you.

**Alison** (*bitterly*) You mean you'd have to get him drunk so he wouldn't know what he was doing? Is that it?

**Frank** That's not it at all, but men talk things over better with a glass of beer in their hands. Anyway—it doesn't matter now, does it, because we've got nothing *to* talk over.

**Alison** (*on the verge of tears*) I'm sorry.

**Frank** Oh, don't worry about it. If you don't want to marry Melvyn, you don't have to, do you? I mean, nobody's going to force you. It's your life. You do what you like with it.

**Alison** (*softly*) Anyway—*he* might not have wanted to marry *me*.

**Frank** Well, that's something we'll never know, isn't it? (*He rises*)

**Alison** I wouldn't mind if you found someone else.

**Frank** Oh, no. I'm finished with it. If you want a husband now, then you'll just have to go out and find one for yourself. Once bitten, twice shy. That's me.

**Alison** I'm sorry, Uncle Frank. I know you were only trying to help me— but *Melvyn.* (*She shakes her head*)

**Frank** Nuff said. The discussion's over.

**Alison** (*tiredly*) I'll get your shirt.

*Alison exits to the parlour*

*Frank looks into the mirror over the fireplace and examines his face as though trying to decide whether to shave or not*

*Alison returns with Frank's shirt*

**Frank** Oh, thanks. (*He begins to put it on*)

**Alison** You—you're not *mad* at me, are you?

**Frank** (*surprised*) Of course I'm not. Every woman's got the right to change her mind. You know that. Now don't think any more about it. It's over and done with, and we can all have a good laugh about it some day, can't we?

*The doorbell chimes*

That'll be Melvyn. Let him in while I finish dressing, will you?

**Alison** What are you going to tell him?

**Frank** Nothing. I'll just take him out for a drink, that's all. (*He smiles at her*) Now go on. Let him in.

*Alison slowly exits to the hall and front door*

*Frank stuffs his shirt into his trousers and turns back to the mirror*

**Peggy** (*off*) Oh, hello, Alison. I hope you don't mind my dropping in like this, but I'd like to see your mother if she's in.

*Frank scowls*

**Alison** (*off*) Come in, Mrs Ramskill. I'll see if I can find her for you.

*Peggy enters from the hall*

**Peggy** (*over her shoulder to Alison*) I only want to see her for a minute, Alison. I won't keep her if she's busy. Hello, Frank. Didn't think *you'd* be in at this time.

**Frank** Just getting ready for the off, Mrs R.

*Alison appears in the arch behind Peggy*

**Peggy** (*moving to the sofa*) We—er—we've heard the news. About Alison.
Jeremy Phillips told us this evening. (*She sits*)

*Alison stays in the arch to listen*

**Frank** (*grimacing*) Of course. (*He strikes his forehead with his clenched fist*)
He works in the *Journal* offices, doesn't he? Blast. (*He grins*) I suppose
he saw that entry form I filled in this afternoon?

**Peggy** (*amused*) Well—the one you *half* filled in. You—er—you forgot to
put down the *groom's* name. (*She laughs*)

**Frank** Oh.

**Peggy** He didn't spot it till after you'd left . . . young Jeremy . . . and he
nearly had a fit. He's so gullible, you know. He really thought it was
genuine. (*She laughs*) It's a good job *I* know you. You and your practical
jokes. Whatever made you think this one up?

**Frank** Well . . . (*He shrugs*)

**Peggy** I don't mind admitting it gave *us* a bit of a shock—for the minute—
till we realized how ridiculous the whole thing was. Until he told us
who'd signed it, we thought it was just a practical joke in very poor
taste. We had a real good laugh about it. All of us.

**Frank** Oh, did you?

**Peggy** Well, of course we did, I mean—how could anybody take a thing
like that *seriously*? But you know—you want to be more careful
about who you play tricks on, Frank Edwards. Especially ones like that
one. It could have been very embarrassing.

**Alison** (*from the arch*) And why's that, Mrs Ramskill? (*She comes down*)

**Peggy** (*turning her head, startled*) Well—it wouldn't have been very nice,
would it? Having nasty rumours spread about you.

**Alison** And what's so nasty about getting married?

**Peggy** (*with half a laugh*) Well—nothing. So long as it's *true*.

**Alison** And what if I told you that it *did* happen to be true?

**Peggy** (*laughing*) Oh, come on, Alison. You didn't even have a boyfriend
this morning, and now you're supposed to be entering the "Bride of the
Year" competition? Honestly. (*She laughs*)

**Frank** Yes, well it's all a mistake . . .

**Alison** (*ignoring him*) I don't find it amusing, Mrs Ramskill. I don't find
it amusing at all.

**Peggy** *We* thought it was hysterical.

**Alison** (*fuming*) Well, I hope you find it just as hysterical when I walk
down the aisle in six weeks' time.

*Frank looks startled*

**Peggy** (*the laugh dying on her lips*) Pardon?

**Alison** (*coldly*) In six weeks' time—at St Catherine's Church—I shall become Mrs Melvyn Thornton—so have a real good laugh about *that*,
Mrs Ramskill.

**Peggy** Melvyn Thornton? You mean Melvyn Thornton from next door?
The one who's not all there? (*She explodes with laughter*) Now I *know*

you're having me on. Oh, dear! (*She mops at her eyes*) You'll have my mascara running in a minute. (*She gurgles with laughter*)

**Alison** (*grimly*) I'll go see if I can find Mother for you.

*Alison turns and marches out upstairs*

**Peggy** (*mopping her eyes again*) Oh, I haven't laughed so much in ages. (*She sniffles*) I suppose you'll be out on the town again, tonight, Frank?

**Frank** That's right. With the future bridegroom. We're going down to the *Horse and Groom* to talk over the wedding plans.

**Peggy** Wedding plans? (*Realization dawning*) You're not *serious*?

**Frank** Perfectly.

**Peggy** (*anxiously*) You mean—she *is* getting married?

**Frank** Like she said. Six weeks' time at St Catherine's.

**Peggy** But she can't! I mean—does Ethel know? Surely *she* doesn't want the girl to saddle herself with a half-wit like Melvyn Thornton?

**Frank** It's nothing to do with her. She's over twenty-one and free to marry anybody that takes her fancy.

**Peggy** (*stunned*) I don't believe it. I just don't believe it.

*Honoria enters from upstairs, carrying a tray with used tea things on it. She deposits this on the drop-leaf table, then turns to look at Peggy. Matilda follows her in with the coats*

**Frank** (*to Honoria*) On your way then, are you?

**Honoria** Early to bed, early to rise.

*Frank helps Honoria on with her coat*

**Frank** That's right. Well, you should just about make it home before the storm breaks.

**Matilda** Into each life a little rain must fall.

**Frank** (*assisting Matilda into her coat*) Yes—I suppose so. You—er—you'll have heard about the wedding plans?

**Honoria** (*sagely*) The best-laid plans of mice and men, gang often go agley.

**Frank** Pardon?

**Matilda** There's many a slip twixt cup and lip.

**Peggy** (*nodding furiously*) And that's just what *I* think too, Mrs . . .?

**Frank** Murchinson. Honoria and Matilda Murchinson. And it's Miss in each case. Aunts—this is Mrs Ramskill. A friend of Ethel's.

*The Aunts incline their heads*

**Peggy** (*indignantly*) They've not even been courting two minutes, and here they are talking about getting married in six weeks. I don't know what the girl's thinking of, I really don't.

**Honoria** It's the early bird that catches the worm.

**Peggy** And look at the worm she's landed. Surely she could have waited a bit longer to see if somebody better came along.

**Matilda** He who hesitates is lost.

**Peggy** (*protesting*) But he hasn't a penny to his name.

**Honoria** Money can't buy happiness.

**Peggy** But at least you can be miserable in comfort, can't you? And you know what they say about love and poverty?

**Matilda** When poverty walks in at the door . . .

**Honoria** Love flies out of the window.

**Peggy** Exactly. You mark my words, Miss Murchinson. That girl will end up having to support *him*. I think she's making a very big mistake.

**Matilda** You can't put an old head on to young shoulders.

**Honoria** You can't make a silk purse out of a sow's ear.

**Peggy** My sentiments, exactly. I can't tell you how surprised *I* am about all this. I mean—she seems such a quiet, sensible girl.

**Matilda** (*nodding*) Still waters run deep.

**Peggy** They certainly do. And especially in her case. We had no idea, Phil and me. No idea at all. We just couldn't believe it when we heard. We thought it was a hoax—we really did. I *was* going to come round in the morning to see if there was anything I could do to help, but I was so worried . . . (*She stops*)

**Honoria** (*nodding*) Never put off till tomorrow what you can do today.

**Peggy** Just what my Phil said—that's my husband, by the way. He keeps the electrical shop in Hagley Street if ever you need anything . . . So I came round right away.

**Frank** Well, now you've got everything off your chest, don't you think you'd better come up with some congratulations for her when she comes back?

**Peggy** Congratulations? Commiserations, more likely. That marriage isn't going to last a week, Frank Edwards, and you know it.

**Frank** It stands as good a chance of lasting as any marriage does these days.

**Peggy** Well, if *that's* what you think, all I can say is you've some funny ideas about marriage. Because when our Edna gets married to Jeremy Phillips, *we* won't be wondering if it's going to last longer than the honeymoon. *They'll* still be married when *their* children are having children.

**Matilda** Don't count your chickens before they're hatched.

**Peggy** (*proudly*) I'm not. He's got a future, Jeremy Phillips has. Assistant Manager now, and with our Edna behind him, he'll be Manager next.

**Honoria** You can lead a horse to water, but you cannot make him drink.

**Peggy** Maybe not, but there's others besides our Edna who'll be keeping an eye on him.

**Matilda** A watched pot never boils.

**Peggy** (*knowingly*) He'll boil all right. You've only got to listen to him talking to know what a marvellous future's in store for him.

**Honoria** An empty vessel makes the loudest noise.

**Frank** Hear, hear.

**Peggy** (*tartly*) Nobody asked for your opinion, Frank Edwards. You've never even met him.

*Ethel enters from upstairs*

**Ethel** Sorry to have kept you waiting, Peggy, but I've been trying to get Aunt Priscilla settled down again.

**Peggy** (*rising*) That's all right, Ethel. (*Coldly*) I've found out what I came round for.

**Ethel** (*apprehensively*) Oh—you've heard then?

**Matilda** Bad news travels fast.

**Ethel** There's no bad news about it, Aunt Matilda. Unexpected, I grant you—but not *bad*.

**Frank** That's right, Sis. You tell them.

**Peggy** (*still frosty*) And when did all this come about, then? You certainly kept very quiet about it this morning, didn't you?

**Ethel** (*uneasily*) Well—it happened just after you'd left, actually.

**Peggy** (*slightly mollified*) A bit sudden, wasn't it?

**Ethel** Yes. It rather took *me* by surprise, too.

**Honoria** Surprise is the best form of attack.

*Peggy stares at Honoria*

**Frank** (*quickly*) She means we sprang it this way to make sure that no-one could copy the wedding plans and lessen the chances of Allison winning the award.

*Peggy's eyebrows rise*

**Peggy** Well, without wishing to appear unkind, Frank—I think that the chances of *that* happening are so remote, you could have had them read on the BBC without losing any sleep over it. She stands about as much chance of winning that title as I do of being Mr Universe. (*To Ethel*) I'm *sorry*, Ethel, but it's no use letting you live in a fool's paradise, is it? Anyway, now that the great secret's out, I don't suppose you'll have any objections to *me* knowing what these mysterious plans are.

**Ethel** (*hesitantly*) Well . . .

**Frank** It's all right, Sis. I'll do it.

*Peggy sits again*

To begin with—the reception's being held at the "Old Tudor Hall" . . .

*Everybody reacts*

**Peggy** (*astounded*) At twelve pounds a head minimum prices?

**Frank** (*beaming*) That's right, Mrs R. And roughly one hundred guests, depending on acceptances. The dress is being designed by Harry Elphinstone, and the honeymoon's in the Canary Islands.

**Peggy** (*stunned*) Harry Elphinstone? Not *the* Harry Elphinstone?

*Frank nods*

But—but that's cheating. She's sure to win if she wears one of his designs. Nobody else is going to stand a chance. (*Outraged*) It's no wonder I'm the last one to know about it. No wonder at all.

**Frank** (*coughing*) Oh, no. You're not the last person to know about it, Mrs R. Not by any means.

**Peggy** (*smarting*) Well, all I can say is "Who is?" then?

*Melvyn appears in the arch. He is smartly dressed but sports a magnificent black eye*

**Melvyn** (*weakly*) The door was open . . .

*Ethel turns away and sinks on to the sofa. Peggy rises in fury*

**Peggy** (*to Melvyn*) You!

*Melvyn looks startled*

You've done this on purpose, haven't you?

**Melvyn** (*touching his eye nervously*) No—it was an accident. Honest.

**Peggy** (*glaring*) Well, if you want a fight, Melvyn Thornton, you can have one with pleasure, because I'll tell you this much for nothing—you'll need more than a fancy wedding dress and a posh dinner to get the best of *me*, you dim-witted—(*she flounders for words*)—worm!

*Peggy snatches up her handbag from the sofa and flounces to the door, exiting through the arch*

**Ethel** (*appealing*) Peggy . . .

**Melvyn** (*bewildered*) Now what did I do wrong?

**Frank** Nothing. She mistook you for somebody else, that's all.

**Melvyn** Oh. (*Quickly*) I'm sorry I'm late, Frank, but I had an accident. (*He touches his eye*)

**Matilda** Better late than never.

*Melvyn glances shyly at the Aunts*

**Honoria** (*looking at Melvyn and then at Matilda*) Like father, like son.

*Matilda nods firmly. Frank looks puzzled*

**Ethel** They met Walter this afternoon.

**Frank** (*realizing*) Oh, I see. (*To Melvyn*) And how come the black eye? Or shouldn't we ask?

**Melvyn** Well—you know that vase I stuck on the front room table? And how it wouldn't come off until it got warmed through—like the cup did? (*He sighs*) I tried to warm it up quickly with the blow-lamp because I was coming out with you, but the flame must have been too strong, or something, and before I knew what was happening, I'd burnt half the table top away.

**Ethel** (*anguished*) Oh, Melvyn.

**Melvyn** I know. There was smoke everywhere—and I couldn't put the flames out.

**Matilda** There's no smoke without fire.

**Melvyn** I tried to do it with the curtains, but they wouldn't come down, so I tried swinging on them and pulling at the same time.

**Honoria** (*nodding*) If at first you don't succeed—try, try again.

**Melvyn** Anyway—they *did* come down then—but I pulled the pelmet out of the wall at the same time—and that's how it happened. My dad was just coming in to see what all the smoke was, and it hit him on the head, knocked him backwards over the sofa and straight through the door of the china cabinet. He was ever so upset about it.

**Ethel** (*softly*) I can't think why?

**Melvyn** And the worse thing about it is the vase is still stuck to the table—and so are the curtains. It's going to cost a fortune to put everything right again.

**Matilda** (*shaking her head*) A fool and his money are soon parted.

**Melvyn** Anyway, my dad says that if he ever catches me experimenting with anything ever again, he's going to break me in little pieces and dance on them. And he gave me this to be going on with. (*He touches his eye gingerly*) You don't think he means it, do you? *Really* means it?

**Honoria** He who pays the piper calls the tune.

**Frank** Well—never mind, Melvyn. You come along with me. We'll go down to the *Horse and Groom* and have a nice quiet drink. You can't get into any scrapes down there.

**Melvyn** (*wryly*) I wouldn't count on that.

**Frank** (*grinning*) I would. It's been standing five hundred years and survived two world wars, so I'm sure you won't be able to do much damage to it. Come on. (*He moves up to the arch*)

**Ethel** (*rising*) I'd better go round and see if there's anything I can do for Walter. (*To the Aunts*) I'll see you to the bus stop, first though. (*She gets her coat from the hall*)

**Frank** We—er—we won't be too late back, Sis. You'll see that everything's ready for us, won't you?

**Ethel** (*appearing with her coat*) I'm having nothing to do with it.

**Frank** Well, in that case, just remind Alison of what I told her this afternoon. (*To Melvyn*) Come on, Mel. (*To the Aunts*) 'Bye.

*Frank and Melvyn exit to the hall*

**Ethel** (*to the Aunts*) Now, have you got everything? Coats, gloves, handbags? All right. We'll get off now or you'll be missing the bus, and I don't think I could stand that on top of everything else.

**Matilda** It's the last straw——

**Honoria** —that breaks the camel's back.

*Ethel rolls her eyes heavenwards, then ushers the Aunts out through the hall*

*There is a moment of silence, then the sound of voices issuing from upstairs*

**Cilla** (*off*) I can do it. I can do it. Let go my arm, child.

**Alison** (*off*) Aunt Cilla—you mustn't.

**Cilla** (*off*) Who says so? Let go.

**Alison** (*off*) You'll *fall*.
**Cilla** (*off*) Not if you stop tugging at me.
**Alison** (*off*) Careful. (*Her voice rising in panic*) Careful!
**Cilla** (*off*) I'm *always* careful. Too careful for my own good.

*Alison appears on the stairs, descending backwards and supporting Aunt Cilla. Aunt Cilla is a frail-looking old lady of about eighty, dressed in a nightgown and shawl and leaning on a stick. She wears a hearing-aid of the old-fashioned kind*

**Alison** (*at the foot of the stairs*) Aunt Cilla, you're not *strong* enough.
**Cilla** (*crossly*) Nonsense, child. Just help me to the chair and stop fussing. I'm not going to fall into pieces.

*Alison helps her to the easy chair, and seats her. Cilla gazes round in disapproval*

Hmmmm. Hasn't altered much, has it? (*She peers at the curtains*) Don't like the curtains.
**Alison** Oh, never mind about the curtains, Aunt Cilla. You shouldn't be down here at all.
**Cilla** Why not? I'm not a prisoner, am I?
**Alison** Of course you aren't. But it's been *years* since you were down here last.
**Cilla** All the more reason for coming down now, then, isn't it?
**Alison** But why? I mean—couldn't you have waited till tomorrow?
**Cilla** No. I might have died during the night.
**Alison** (*laughing*) You're not going to die. Not for a long time yet.
**Cilla** (*grunting*) Glad to hear it. Taken up forecasting the future now, have you?
**Alison** (*smiling*) No. It's just that you're like the original creaking gate. You'll be a long time falling off.
**Cilla** (*waspishly*) Go wash your mouth out with soap. Go on. Right this minute.
**Alison** (*startled*) Why? What have I said?
**Cilla** I won't have you quoting proverbs at me. I've stood it for over fifty-seven years from that pair of doddering idiots, but I'm sure I'm not going to endure it from you as well.
**Alison** (*contritely*) Sorry.
**Cilla** I should think so, too. Two fools in one family are enough for anybody to cope with. (*Her eyes twinkling*) Now make me a nice cup of tea, and you can give me all the details of the wedding without interruption.
**Alison** I could have told you those upstairs.
**Cilla** I know you could—but they'll sound a lot better down here.
**Alison** How can they?
**Cilla** Because I'll turn my deaf-aid louder. Now go and make me that tea.
**Alison** (*resignedly*) All right.

*Alison exits to the kitchen*

**Cilla** (*calling*) And don't be frightened to put some tea in the pot, either. (*She mutters*) I've not had a decent cup since I went up those stairs six years ago.

*There is a knock at the back door, which she ignores*

It's all these tea-bags, nowadays. Sweepings-up in paper packets and not a scrap of taste in them. (*She grimaces*)

*Walter appears in the archway, a bandage tied roughly round his head and his arm in a sling. He sees Cilla and coughs with embarrassment*

**Walter** Oh—excuse me. I was looking for Ethel.

*Cilla turns, startled, and gazes at him*

**Cilla** Oh? Well, she's out. (*She peers at him closely*) And what have *you* been up to? Fighting?
**Walter** Eh? Oh—no. No. Just a bit of a mishap, that's all.
**Cilla** Mishap my foot. Somebody's been trying to brain you. Who was it? Jealous husband?
**Walter** (*startled*) No. No, of course it wasn't.
**Cilla** There's no "of course" about it. It *could* have been. My Arnold was a jealous husband. Once frightened the life out of some young chap who'd been making eyes at me over a glass of home-made wine—and I was fifty-nine then. (*She laughs*) Jealous till the day he died, my Arnold. The great fool.

*Alison enters from the kitchen*

**Alison** Who are you talking to? (*She sees Walter*) Oh, Mr Thornton. You're hurt.
**Walter** (*relieved to see her*) Just a few scratches, that's all.
**Cilla** (*sitting up*) Thornton? Walter Thornton is it? From next door? The one who sends the flowers?
**Walter** That's me. Yes.
**Cilla** (*holding out her hand*) Priscilla Murchinson.
**Walter** (*taking it*) You mean—you're Aunt Cilla? From upstairs?
**Cilla** As ever was. (*She pumps his hand*)
**Walter** Well, by heck.
**Cilla** (*eagerly*) Come on. Sit down. (*She pulls him on to the chair arm*) Alison, bring a cup of tea for Walter, as well. He looks as though he could use it.
**Walter** (*heavily*) I wouldn't turn it down, that's for sure.
**Alison** I'll bring one through with ours.
**Cilla** (*indicating his injuries*) And how did this lot happen, then? Took a tumble, did you?

**Walter** No. The pelmet fell on my head, that's all, and I turned my wrist by trying to put it back where it belonged.

**Cilla** You'd never get one of those things back on to the wall by yourself.

**Walter** I wasn't trying to. I was attempting to shove it down somebody's throat.

*Alison grimaces*

**Cilla** I see.

**Walter** That's another fifty pounds' damage done by my estimates. No wonder I'm always broke.

**Cilla** That'll be your son again, I'm thinking. Melvyn. (*Brightly*) Well, never mind. It won't be your problem for much longer, will it?

*Walter looks surprised. Alison is alarmed*

**Alison** Aunt Cilla . . .

**Cilla** You'll soon have him off your hands. (*She beams at him*)

**Alison** (*quickly*) Isn't it time you were going back upstairs?

**Cilla** I've only just come down them. Besides, I've spent six years up there. I might just decide to spend the next six down here.

**Walter** (*curiously*) What do you mean—when he's off my hands?

**Cilla** After the wedding.

**Alison** Aunt Cilla, Please . . .

**Walter** Wedding?

**Cilla** (*sharply*) Oh, stop fussing, child, and go see if the kettle is boiling. (*To Walter*) Yes. The wedding. (*She pokes him with her finger*) I bet you never expected to get an old busybody like me for an in-law when you started coming round here, did you? (*She beams*) Yes—it'll be nice having you in the family. I like you. You can bring me flowers every day, then.

**Walter** (*embarrassed*) Oh—it's not gone as far as that yet, Mrs Murchinson. It's just friendship.

**Cilla** (*surprised*) Friendship? (*To Alison*) But I thought you said all the plans had been made?

**Walter** There must be some mistake. I—er—I've not even broached the subject with her, let alone made plans. (*He shakes his head*) By heck, but you're a sharp one, you are. I didn't think it showed.

**Cilla** It doesn't. I don't know what you're talking about.

**Walter** (*puzzled*) Well—me and Ethel.

**Cilla** You and Ethel? I'm talking about your Melvyn.

**Alison** (*weakly*) I'll go and make that tea. (*She moves to the kitchen door*)

**Cilla** I was saying that you wouldn't have to worry about the damage after he's got himself married.

**Walter** Married? Our Melvyn? That'll be the day.

**Cilla** (*surprised*) You mean—you don't *know* about it?

*Alison cringes*

*Ethel enters from the hall in a fluster*

**Ethel** Alison. I've just been next door and . . . (*She sees Walter*) Walter.

*Walter rises from the chair arm*

Oh, what a mess you're in. Let me have a . . . (*She sees Cilla*) Aunt Cilla. What on earth are *you* doing down here?

**Cilla** Snooping.

**Alison** I'm sorry, Mum, but she insisted on coming down.

**Ethel** (*dropping her coat on the sofa back*) All right. Now come on. Back to bed with you *right now*. (*She moves to Cilla*) Take her other arm, Alison.

**Cilla** (*protesting*) I don't want to go back upstairs. I want to stay here. Besides—I want my cup of tea.

**Ethel** (*firmly*) I'll bring it up to you.

**Cilla** (*determined*) No. I don't see why I should miss all the fun—and anyway—it's always cold by the time you get to my room.

**Ethel** That's not true, Aunt Cilla, and you know it. It's perfectly hot.

**Cilla** How do you know? You don't have to drink it.

**Ethel** (*giving in*) Oh, all right. You can have it down here, then it's straight up to bed with you. You shouldn't be down here at all at this time of night.

**Cilla** Why not? There's nothing wrong with me. Don't want me dropping dead in the living-room, is that it?

**Ethel** (*laughing*) Honestly. (*To Alison*) Is the kettle on?

**Alison** (*nodding*) Should have boiled by now. I'll make the tea.

**Ethel** No, I'll do it. Oh—and by the way—(*she glances at Walter*)—Frank says to remind you of what he told you this afternoon—whatever *that* means. Won't be a minute, Walter, then I'll look at those bandages for you.

*Ethel exits to the kitchen*

**Alison** Would you like me to do them, Mr Thornton?

**Walter** I'll be all right. There's no need to fuss.

**Alison** (*desperately*) I'll do them if you like.

**Walter** No, no. I'll be fine.

**Cilla** Leave the poor man alone, can't you? We were just talking about . . .

*Ethel enters with the tea things on a tray*

**Ethel** I've made the tea. (*She puts the tray on the coffee-table and moves back to the kitchen*) Set the cups, will you, love?

*Ethel exits to the kitchen*

*Alison moves over to the coffee-table*

**Walter** (*to Cilla*) About this wedding . . . ?
**Alison** (*brightly*) You do take milk and sugar, don't you, Mr Thornton?
**Walter** Yes please. Just two spoons. (*To Cilla*) You were saying?

*Ethel enters with the teapot*

**Ethel** Tea up. Just half a cup for Aunt Cilla. (*She pours*)
**Cilla** (*peering at the liquid*) Tea-bags again.
**Ethel** (*continuing pouring*) I'll run a bowl of water for your head, Walter.
   (*She hands the cup to Alison for Walter*)
**Walter** Oh, you needn't bother. (*He takes the cup*) Thank you.
**Alison** (*handing a second cup to Cilla*) Aunt. (*She returns to the table*)
**Ethel** I'll get that water now.

*Ethel exits to the kitchen*

**Cilla** (*puzzled*) Set *what* shorter?
**Walter** Eh? (*He realizes*) Oh, no. She said she'd get that *water*.
**Cilla** Oh—for your head. Yes. (*She raps her hearing-aid in annoyance*)
**Walter** Something wrong?

*Alison looks up and watches them*

**Cilla** Wrong? No. No, I think the batteries are going, that's all.
**Walter** Have you got spares? I'll fit them for you if you have.
**Cilla** (*frowning*) Chairs?
**Walter** (*louder*) Spares. (*He indicates the hearing-aid*) New batteries.
**Cilla** (*baffled*) New bath is here?
**Walter** (*louder still*) Battery.
**Cilla** Flattery? (*He laughs*) Yes. Yes. But it won't do you any good. I can
   hardly hear a thing now. (*She raps the hearing-aid again*)

*Ethel enters with a bowl of water*

**Ethel** Something the matter?
**Walter** Her batteries have gone.
**Ethel** Oh, dear. And they were the last ones. I clean forgot to pick up the
   others today, what with all the worry about Alison. (*She puts the bowl
   down on the floor near the sofa*) I'd better take her back upstairs. She'll
   not be able to hear a thing and she'll only start fretting. (*To Cilla*) Come
   on, Auntie. I'll take you back up.
**Cilla** Tobacco?
**Ethel** (*pointing upwards*) Back up. Upstairs. Up.
**Cilla** (*annoyed*) Oh, all right. I can't hear a thing anybody's saying, anyway.

*With the help of Ethel, Walter and Alison, she is assisted to her feet*

   Good night, Mr Thornton. I'll see you tomorrow, I expect.
**Walter** (*loudly*) Good night.

**Ethel** I'll be down in a minute, Walter.

*Ethel exits with Cilla to go upstairs*

**Alison** I—I suppose *I'd* better go get ready, too.
**Walter** (*surprised*) Going out, are you?
**Alison** Well—not exactly. I—er—I'm expecting someone. A friend.
**Walter** (*nodding*) Oh.
**Alison** You will excuse me, won't you, Mr Thornton?
**Walter** Course I will. I'll be all right till your mother gets back. Off you go.

*Alison smiles at him in a strange, half embarrassed way, then exits quickly upstairs*

(*Looking after her*) Wonder what's making *her* so nervous? (*He takes a step back to turn and puts his foot in the bowl of water*) Ohhhh! That's all I needed. (*He lifts his sopping wet foot out of the bowl and sits on the sofa to remove his shoe and sock*)

*As he is doing this, Frank appears in the arch. He is coatless, his shirt is crumpled and torn. His face and hair are smothered in dirt and straw, and a large bruise is forming just below his eye. His breath comes in agonized gasps*

Frank! (*He rises*) What the devil have you been up to, lad?
**Frank** (*weakly*) Just a slight accident. (*He totters to the sofa and collapses on it*)
**Walter** (*heavily*) It's not the first time he's been called that. What's he done now?
**Frank** It wasn't *his* fault *this* time. Not really.
**Walter** (*tiredly*) It doesn't have to be. He's a walking disaster area. Come on. Let me know the worst. How can a quiet drink in the local pub develop into this? (*He indicates Frank*)
**Frank** (*wincing*) Well, actually—it all started *before* we got inside. Just as we'd got to the door, in fact. (*He stops*)
**Walter** Go on.
**Frank** I'm trying to get it all in sequence. It all happened so fast. I've never seen anything like it before. (*Pause*) Well, what happened was—(*he winces*)—you know there's the two stone steps you go up to get to the main door: the one by the car-park? And the door's one of those double hinge types. Push and pull?
**Walter** (*nodding*) Aye. Stupid things they are.
**Frank** Well that was it. Melvyn was going in first, and instead of pushing the door—he pulled it. It smacked him straight on the nose and stubbed his toes at the same time.

*Walter shakes his head, eyes closed*

Anyway—there he was—hopping up and down on one leg and clutching his nose and his foot—when somebody *inside* gave the door a shove and knocked him flying off the steps head first through the windscreen of an Anglia parked at the side. Of course—the blasted thing *would* have to be fitted with an alarm, and off it went. The chap it belonged to must have heard it, because he came rushing out like a mad bull and found me trying to get Melvyn out. Without waiting to ask questions, he landed this on me—(*he touches his eye*)—and knocked me half senseless. By the time I'd got to my feet again, he'd picked Melvyn up and flung him up the steps again and straight through the pub doors. And that's when the fun *really* started.

**Walter** You mean there's more to come?

**Frank** (*nodding wearily*) You know that pile of pennies they had on the bar counter? For the Spastic Society?

**Walter** (*wincing*) Oh, no. He didn't.

**Frank** (*nodding*) He did. Hit it like a ball hitting ninepins, and the whole lot went for a Burton. All five and a half hundredweight of it. We heard the crash from the car-park.

**Walter** (*groaning*) No.

**Frank** I've not finished yet. You haven't heard the worst. There I was in the car-park, with this madman still trying to beat me to a pulp and the car alarm screaming its knickers off—when we heard the second crash.

**Walter** Second one?

**Frank** (*nodding*) The one that came when the roof caved in.

**Walter** (*his eyes widening*) Eh?

**Frank** It was like something from a silent movie. You see—when the coins went over, they crashed into that wooden beam at the other end of the counter—the one that held the centre roof beam in position. It must have been put there in Elizabeth the First's time, and when all that lot crashed into it, the thing just snapped in two. It must have been rotten with age and the shock was too much for it. So the roof came in.

**Walter** (*stunned*) It's not possible. It's just not possible.

**Frank** Of course, we dashed into the place to see what had happened, but it was absolute chaos. Everybody was screaming blue murder and there was soot and plaster and thatching all over. It was like a battlefield.

**Walter** (*anxiously*) There was nobody injured, was there?

**Frank** (*shaking his head*) Fortunately the place wasn't too full . . . and a good job, too, because we hadn't been inside two seconds before the splintering started.

**Walter** No. I don't want to hear any more.

**Frank** (*continuing*) That must have been the beams in the cellar going, because there was another crash as the brickwork collapsed and the floor gave a lurch. Everybody made a dash for the doors, and we just got out before the whole lot caved in.

**Walter** (*covering his ears and closing his eyes*) No, no, no.

**Frank** Then to cap it all—two of the walls came down as well. It was all over in five minutes, and the place is a complete wreck.

**Walter** (*after a stunned and deathly pause*) That's it, then. I'm finished. I can't take any more. I haven't the money or anything. I'm done for.

**Frank** It's not your fault, Walter. It was an accident. Pure and simple. They can't blame Melvyn for this. It could have happened at any time.

**Walter** (*tiredly*) Maybe—but it's happened *now*—and it was our Melvyn who caused it. (*He rises*) Where is he now? At home?

**Frank** They took him to the hospital with the others. For shock. Don't worry. I think I got the worst of it with this eye. (*He touches it and winces*)

**Walter** You'd best let Ethel take a look at it.

**Frank** It'll be all right. I've had worse. (*Grinning*) We're going to look a right trio, aren't we? One with a black eye, one with a busted nose and a stubbed toe, and one with a cracked skull and a sprained wrist.

**Walter** He'll have more than a busted nose and a stubbed toe when I've finished with him. He's really gone and done it now. He got a warning from the police last time with his gas explosions but this time it'll be a jail sentence.

**Frank** Don't be daft, Walter. It was an accident.

**Walter** That's as maybe—but that pub was listed as an Ancient Monument. Remember the fuss they created when the owners wanted to fit them swing-doors and modernize the place? It almost took an Act of Parliament before they could replace a floorboard. (*He shakes his head*) He'll go down for twenty years for this lot. Thank goodness his mother's not alive to see it. (*He sighs*) I'd best get off down to the police station and see what's going to happen next.

**Frank** They said they'd be taking statements tomorrow, but you don't have to worry. I've already told them it wasn't his fault.

**Walter** Thanks, Frank. But there's been that many complaints . . . (*He moves to the arch*)

*Ethel enters from upstairs*

**Ethel** (*surprised*) You're not going, are you? (*She sees Frank*) Frank! What on earth have you been up to?

**Walter** (*bitterly*) Need you ask? It's Melvyn again.

**Ethel** You mean—he *hit* you? (*She stares at Frank in disbelief*)

**Walter** No. He's just demolished the *Horse and Groom*. I'm going down to the police station now.

**Ethel** (*wide-eyed*) Demolished? (*She looks from one to the other*)

**Walter** Frank'll explain to you. I'll perhaps be back later—unless they lock *me* up as well.

**Ethel** Just a minute. I'll get my coat. I'm coming with you. (*She picks up her coat*)

**Frank** There's no need, Sis. Everything's all right. Honest it is.

**Ethel** (*firmly*) If Walter's going down to the police station, then I'm going with him. I want to know exactly what's happened.

**Frank** I'll tell you.

**Ethel** *Walter* can tell me. He's not going down there on his own in his condition, and that's final. I don't want him passing out in the street.

**Walter** I'll be all right, Ethel.

**Ethel** I'm coming with you. (*To Frank*) And I shall want a few words with *you*, Frank Edwards, as soon as I get back. Understand? (*To Walter*) Come along, Walter.

*Ethel leads Walter firmly out through the hall*

*Frank stands gloomily gazing after them, then turns back into the room*

**Frank** And I can guess what *that* means.

*Melvyn enters through the kitchen door. He wears a tattered filthy shirt, bloodstained at the front. His trousers are ripped to the knee, and he wears only one shoe. His face is soot smeared and his black eye and bloodied nose are framed by his matted hair*

**Melvyn** (*timidly*) Hello.

**Frank** (*spinning round*) Melvyn—I thought you'd gone to the hospital?

**Melvyn** I did—but the ambulance ran into a road-up sign in Market Street, so I decided to come back home instead.

**Frank** Your dad's just gone down to the police station.

**Melvyn** I know. I heard you talking to him before he went.

**Frank** You mean you've been in the kitchen all the time?

**Melvyn** Only the last few minutes. I couldn't get in our house because I've lost my key, so I came round here the back way.

**Frank** Why didn't you come in?

**Melvyn** I didn't want my dad to see me like this. (*He sits in the easy chair despairingly*) You don't have a gun I could borrow for a few minutes, do you? I want to shoot myself.

**Frank** Cheer up, Melvyn. Like I told your dad, it wasn't your fault this time. They can't blame you.

**Melvyn** (*gloomily*) It's no good, Frank. It *was* my fault—as usual. I'm no use to anybody, am I? I'm just a mess.

**Frank** (*laughing despite himself*) You certainly are at the minute. Come on. We'd better see if we can do anything about you. Get your clothes off and I'll see if I can find something of mine to fit you. You can't wander round looking like that. You can wash off in the kitchen.

**Melvyn** (*rising*) I'm sorry, Frank.

*Frank looks at him amusedly, shakes his head and exits upstairs*

*Melvyn catches sight of himself in the mirror and crosses to it to have a closer look*

Ooooh. (*He gingerly touches his nose, yelps and drops his hand. Turning, he spots the bowl of water on the floor. Fishing a handkerchief from his pocket, he dips the end in the water and applies it to his face, peering into the mirror as he does so*) Oww! Oh, I've really gone and done it this time. (*He yelps*) He's going to kill me. (*Turning from the mirror, he attempts to brush himself down with his hand to no avail*) I suppose I *could* join the Foreign Legion. At least I won't be able to do much damage out there in the desert. Not with all that sand and nothing else. (*He sits on the sofa*) Still—with my luck, they'd probably have a plague of Date Blight and blame me for it. (*He sinks his head in his hands*)

*Frank enters with a sweater and slacks*

**Frank** Here you are. Put these on. You can change in the front room. I'll just go and get out of these things, and I'll be back in a minute or two. Okay?

**Melvyn** *taking the things*) Thanks. (*He rises but does not move*)

**Frank** I'd better get rid of this. (*He picks up the bowl*) Well—go on.

**Melvyn** There—there's nothing in there that's breakable, is there?

**Frank** (*thinking*) I don't think so—only the standard lamp. But you won't be going near that. It's at the far end of the room.

**Melvyn** I just thought I'd better make certain.

*Melvyn exits to the parlour*

**Frank** (*pushing open the kitchen door and calling*) Light switch is by the door . . .

*There is a shattering crash from the parlour*

(*Groaning*) Oh, no.

*Melvyn enters, holding his nose*

**Melvyn** I tripped over the carpet.

**Frank** (*tiredly*) I should have known. Have you broken it?

**Melvyn** I don't think so. It's just a bit sore. (*He touches his nose*)

**Frank** (*patiently*) I meant the standard lamp.

**Melvyn** (*realizing*) Oh—no. No. The standard lamps all right. It wasn't damaged at all.

**Frank** (*relieved*) Thank the Lord for that.

**Melvyn** It was the television set that fell over.

*Frank reels*

(*Quickly*) But don't worry, Frank. It's only a leg that's snapped off. I'll fix it for you as soon as I've got changed. It won't take me a minute.

**Frank** No—I mean—no, it doesn't matter, Melvyn. Just leave the pieces where they are and I'll sort them out later. Just get changed and get back in here, I—er—I want to have a quiet word with you.

*Melvyn nods, and exits to the parlour*

*Frank stands for a moment listening for the crash, but there is absolute silence. He takes the bowl to the kitchen, then goes to the parlour door*

(*Calling*) How are you doing?
**Melvyn** (*off*) Won't be a minute.

*Alison appears on the stairs moving down. She wears an evening gown, well-dressed wig, and is made up with a pleasing effect. She has also removed her spectacles and is therefore as blind as a bat. She fumbles her way into the room*

**Alison** (*nervously*) Frank? Are you there?
**Frank** (*turning*) Alison.
**Alison** How do I look? (*She moves down blindly*)
**Frank** (*delighted*) Like an *angel*.
**Alison** (*sadly*) I knew it. Like nothing on earth.
**Frank** No, I mean it. You look *fantastic*. Stunning. Honestly.
**Alison** I'm so *nervous*.
**Frank** (*embracing her*) You'll knock him for six.
**Alison** He's not arrived yet, has he? (*She peers round myopically*)
**Frank** He's in the parlour. Taking his things off.
**Alison** (*startled*) Eh?
**Frank** (*laughing*) It's all right. He's had another accident, that's all, and torn his trousers. I've lent him a pair of mine. He'll be out in a minute.
**Alison** (*anxiously*) What did you say to him? About proposing.
**Frank** Oh—well—as a matter of fact—I haven't had time to say anything to him as yet.
**Alison** (*horrified*) What?
**Frank** But don't worry. I'll have a word with him now. As soon as he comes out.
**Alison** (*panic stricken*) But you can't. Not now. Not while *I'm* here. (*She turns*) Where's the archway? (*She staggers forwards*)
**Frank** (*grabbing her arm*) Calm down, will you? Of course I'm not going to say anything with you here. Nip into the kitchen and put the kettle on or something, and I'll give you a call when I've got everything sorted out.
**Alison** No. I can't go through with it, Uncle Frank. It's all been a mistake. I mean—I just can't.
**Frank** Now don't start all that again. There's nothing to worry about. Off you go and leave everything to me.
**Alison** (*trembling*) All right. (*She moves behind the easy chair with arms outstretched, towards the parlour door*)
**Frank** (*turning away and not noticing this*) You'll spend the rest of your life thanking me for this.

*Alison exits into the parlour. There is a yell from Melvyn. Alison comes blundering out as Frank spins round*

**Alison** Uncle Frank! (*She staggers blindly in*) Uncle Frank.
**Frank** (*grabbing her*) It's all right. It's all right. I've got you.

*Melvyn enters from the parlour*

**Melvyn** I was just pulling my trousers up.
**Frank** It's all right, Melvyn. You startled her, that's all. There's no harm done.
**Melvyn** (*staring at Alison*) I'm ever so sorry, Alison.
**Alison** (*smiling weakly at the easy chair*) That's all right, Melvyn.
**Melvyn** That's a nice dress you've got on, isn't it?
**Alison** Oh. Thank you.
**Melvyn** You look ever so pretty.
**Alison** (*attempting to smile*) Do I? Must be an accident.

*Frank helps Alison to the sofa, where she sits*

**Melvyn** I wouldn't say that, Alison. I think you're pretty all the time.
**Alison** (*nonplussed*) Oh—well thank you.
**Melvyn** I—er—I haven't seen you look like this before, have I?
**Alison** No.
**Melvyn** It's not really you though, is it?
**Alison** (*shaking her head*) Not really.
**Melvyn** I like you better as you are usually.
**Frank** (*astounded*) Well, I like that!
**Melvyn** (*quickly*) I didn't mean . . .
**Alison** It's all right, Melvyn. I think *I* like myself better the other way, too. This is just—sort of an *experiment*.
**Melvyn** Oh. (*There is a slight pause*) Alison?
**Alison** Mmmmm?
**Melvyn** Would you—would you mind if—if—if I *asked* you some—thing?
**Alison** (*after a slight pause*) What?
**Melvyn** (*glancing at Frank*) Well—something—something *personal*.
**Alison** (*puzzled*) It all depends.
**Melvyn** (*to Frank*) Would you mind? If I just had a little talk with her—on my own? I want some advice, you see.
**Frank** From Alison? Can't *I* help you?
**Melvyn** No. It has to be woman's advice.
**Frank** (*shrugging*) All right. But don't take too long. I still want to have a talk with you about another personal matter. I'll go up and change.

*Frank exits upstairs*

**Melvyn** (*sitting beside Alison*) You don't mind, do you?
**Alison** Well—I won't know till I know what sort of advice you want, will I?
**Melvyn** (*gulping*) It's about a girl. Somebody very special. In fact—it's a girl I've fallen in love with.

**Alison** (*stunned*) Oh.

**Melvyn** (*quickly*) You don't mind me asking you, do you, but I don't know what to do about it. I don't know much about girls, you see, and you're the only person I know who might be able to help me.

**Alison** Me? You mean . . . you want some advice from *me*? Of all people. (*She begins to laugh almost hysterically*)

**Melvyn** (*bewildered*) Have I said something wrong?

**Alison** (*trying to get a hold on herself*) No. No. It's all right, Melvyn. Go on. Ask me what you want to know, and I'll try to help you.

**Melvyn** (*glancing uneasily at her*) Well, you see. I'm not good looking, and no girl in her right mind would want to be seen dead in my company because everything I touch seems to fall to pieces—but I've fallen in love with this one and I can't sleep at nights for thinking about her.

**Alison** I see.

**Melvyn** That's the reason all my experiments are going wrong. I just can't seem to concentrate on them. All I do is think about her and then my mind starts wandering and—boom. (*He throws his hands up*)

**Alison** Does she know how you feel about her?

**Melvyn** No. She's no idea at all. If only I could pluck up enough courage to tell her—even if she told me to go take a running jump at myself— well it would settle the matter one way or another, wouldn't it?

**Alison** I suppose so.

**Melvyn** So I thought you might be able to advise me how to go about it, so to speak. I've not had much experience with girls—not any, to be truthful—and I don't know what to say. I'll never have another chance like this one—not with a girl like her—but I'm terrified of saying anything to her. (*Anxiously*) You don't think I'm making a fool of myself, do you?

**Alison** (*rising*) No, Melvyn. I know just how you must be feeling. And if you are making a fool of yourself—well that makes two of us.

**Melvyn** Oh? Are you in love, too?

**Alison** (*sadly*) No. I'm not in love. I'm not anything.

**Melvyn** (*anxiously*) You didn't mind my asking, did you? It's just that— well—I think I've got as much right to happiness as anybody else, haven't I?

**Alison** There's no such thing as "right to happiness", Melvyn. If you want happiness in this life, you've got to fight for it. It's no use sitting at home and waiting for it to find you. You've got to go out and meet it half way. It's like the Aunts are so fond of saying: "Nothing ventured, nothing gained."

**Melvyn** (*rising*) Do you really mean that? Honestly?

**Alison** (*nodding to hide her tears*) Don't let it slip through your fingers. You might never get the chance again.

**Melvyn** I'm glad you said that, Alison. It's helped me to make my mind up at last. I'll propose to her tonight, shall I? After all—she can only say yes or no, can't she?

**Alison** That's right, Melvyn. (*She turns away*)

**Melvyn** (*quietly*) Will you marry me, Alison?

*There is a stunned silence. Alison turns slowly*

**Alison** (*softly*) What did you say?

**Melvyn** Will you marry me? (*Quickly*) You don't have to say anything right now if you'd rather think it over first, but if you will marry me then the plans can go ahead for the wedding and things, and we can live next door with my dad, and you can always come home again if you get tired of me, and . . .

**Alison** (*cutting in*) Melvyn. Melvyn. You mean—you're asking me to marry you? To actually *marry* you?

**Melvyn** Well—yes. Oh, I know you're not in love with *me*, but I've been in love with you ever since we moved in next door, and I know that if you *will* marry me, you might come to like me just a little bit, later on, and I'd do anything for you. Honestly I would.

**Alison** (*stunned*) You're quite serious? I mean—serious?

**Melvyn** (*nodding*) I know I'm not a very good catch, but—well—will you?

**Alison** Yes, Melvyn. I will. (*She bursts into tears and sits*)

*Frank enters downstairs*

**Frank** What's going on?

**Alison** (*sobbing*) We're going to be married—and I'm so happy.

*Alison continues to sob wildly, as—*

the CURTAIN *falls*

SCENE 2

*The same. Saturday morning, six weeks later*

*The room is neat and tidy, apart from various brightly wrapped boxes and parcels which obviously contain wedding gifts. Congratulatory cards are also very much in evidence. The fire is lit and burning brightly. The room curtains are open, but the main light is on. The reason for this is the weather. Outside it is black as pitch, torrential rain is falling, and distant thunder, followed by flashes of lightning, can be seen*

*Aunt Cilla, resplendent in her wedding clothes, is sitting calmly on the sofa, the ghost of a smile playing around her lips. Peggy, in a smart, dark-coloured two-piece, is standing by the window looking out. There is a moment's silence, then Peggy speaks without turning*

**Peggy** Well—I can't see this lot doing anything to improve her chances, can you? It hasn't let up since half past four this morning.

**Cilla** Oh? And how would you know?

**Peggy** I was awake, wasn't I? Couldn't sleep a wink with all that thunder crashing and the rain beating on the bedroom windows. I don't think anybody could—except Phil. I had to wake him up to show him.

**Cilla** You're quite sure it wasn't something *else* that kept you awake, are you? Like a guilty conscience, for instance.

**Peggy** (*turning in surprise*) What should *I* have a guilty conscience about?

**Cilla** I wouldn't know—but you might have spent the last six weeks praying it would rain like this today, for all I know.

**Peggy** (*with a half laugh*) Really. If you're referring to that little incident a few weeks ago . . .

**Cilla** Well, yes. I must confess I was.

**Peggy** It's all over and done with. I *was* a bit upset—as I told Ethel last night. It was only natural. After all, I *am* her closest friend, when all's said and done, and I felt rather hurt that she didn't see fit to let me in on the big secret. Of course, once I'd cooled down a bit and begun to think about it—well, I realized what a fool I'd made of myself. (*She moves behind the easy chair*) That's why I haven't been round before. I just couldn't face anybody. But as for praying for rain—well, really.

**Cilla** Hmm. Well, I suppose that's your story, and you'll be sticking to it.

**Peggy** What else can I say? (*She looks round*) Er—these aren't *all* the wedding presents, are they?

**Cilla** No. Most of them have gone down to the reception hall. Why?

**Peggy** Well, I was wondering. I—er—I can't see that little lamp that Phil and I sent over, that's all.

**Cilla** Oh, yes. The gold lamp with the red shade.

**Peggy** That's the one. Did you like it?

**Cilla** Yes. It looked quite nice.

**Peggy** I—er—I shouldn't really tell you this—(*she glances round to make sure no-one else could be listening*)—but it ran *quite* expensive. Much more expensive than it actually looks.

**Cilla** So I noticed.

*Peggy looks puzzled*

You left the price ticket stuck to the base.

**Peggy** (*aghast*) I *didn't.* (*Annoyed*) That means everybody will have seen how much we paid for it.

**Cilla** No it doesn't. I took it off. Nobody saw it but me.

*Peggy's face is a picture of frustrated disappointment*

**Peggy** (*recovering*) Mind you—it's a beautiful little lamp. I wouldn't have minded keeping it for myself. (*She bridles*)

**Cilla** Why didn't you? Or better still—if you like it so much—why don't you buy another one?

**Peggy** At that price? (*She raises her eyebrows*)

**Cilla** Oh, no. I wasn't suggesting you paid anything like *that* price. I've seen the identical thing in your shop for eight pounds *less*.

*Peggy looks startled*

I called in yesterday afternoon for new batteries and saw them on the counter. Little gold table lamps with red shades. Marked down for quick sale, I believe the notice said.

**Peggy** (*confused*) Oh—you must have been mistaken, Mrs Murchinson. I mean—you've seen the price tag on *ours*, haven't you? *And* the store card.

**Cilla** Store card? No. I didn't notice the store card.

**Peggy** Well it was *there*. Stuck to the base. Right next to the pri—— (*She breaks off*)

**Cilla** Yes. Right next to the price tag. (*She smiles sweetly*)

**Peggy** (*turning back to the window in some confusion*) Listen to that *rain*. Poor Alison's going to look like a drowned rat by the time she gets to the church doors. I mean—an umbrella's not going to keep this lot off her, is it? And I shudder to think what'll happen if anybody's daft enough to throw confetti at her. We all know what that's like when it's wet. It sticks like glue and all the colour runs.

**Cilla** I don't think we need worry about that too much, Mrs Ramskill.

**Peggy** (*turning to stare at her*) On a white wedding dress?

**Cilla** There'll be no wet confetti on her wedding dress. Not today.

**Peggy** (*baffled*) I don't understand.

*Ethel enters from upstairs. She wears a new skirt and blouse, and looks flustered*

**Ethel** (*to Cilla*) Hasn't Mr Elphinstone arrived with the dress yet? Hello, Peggy. I didn't know you'd arrived. You will excuse me, won't you? (*She flutters helplessly*)

**Peggy** Of course I will. (*She smiles*)

**Cilla** No. There's been nobody since this one. (*She indicates Peggy*)

**Peggy** (*ignoring this*) How's it going, Ethel?

**Ethel** It's not. (*She turns her eyes heavenwards*) It's utter bedlam. Frank's in the bathroom and no-one else can get in. He's been locked in there for the last hour babbling something to himself and refusing to answer me or open the door. Alison seems to be in a state of shock, and she's done nothing but cry since the day before yesterday. Her hair's in a mess and I can't do a thing with it. I've knocked the nail varnish all over the bedroom carpet. The dress hasn't arrived—and neither have the Aunts. I told them to be here for ten o'clock, and here we are at nearly half past with still no sign. We're due at the church in an hour and we're nowhere *near* ready. And look at the weather . . .

**Peggy** Never mind, Ethel. It does the groom good to be kept waiting.

**Ethel** Maybe . . . but that doesn't apply to Melvyn. If he's in that church five minutes before *we* are, there'll be no building left standing to have the wedding in. (*She shakes her head*) Oh dear, I do hope she's doing the right thing.

**Cilla** She will. Now stop fluttering round like a mother hen. Everything will go off with a bang.

**Ethel** With Melvyn around, that's what I'm afraid of.

**Peggy** He was very lucky over that court case, wasn't he? He could have been in jail by now if things had gone the other way.

**Cilla** (*fiercely*) Rubbish. It was an accident. Pure and simple. Even the owners said so. Could have happened at any time and to anybody. That's why it wasn't taken any further. It should never have gone to court anyway.

**Peggy** They didn't have much choice, did they? After all—it was an Ancient Monument.

**Cilla** (*sourly*) So am I. But they won't take anybody to court for knocking *me* down.

**Ethel** You'll have to excuse me, Peggy. I've still got a thousand and one things to do. If you want a drink, just help yourself. It's all in the kitchen.

**Peggy** You're sure there's nothing I can do to help?

**Ethel** Just let me know the minute the dress arrives. (*She hurries out to the stairs*)

*The doorbell chimes*

(*Calling*) It's probably the Aunts, at last. Be a love and let them in, Peggy.

*Ethel exits upstairs*

**Peggy** (*to Cilla*) Is there somewhere I can put the coats to dry?

**Cilla** (*ignoring her and fumbling with her hearing-aid*) Where's that off switch?

*Peggy glowers at her for a moment, then exits to the hall*

*Cilla switches off and leans back with a smile of pleasure*

**Peggy** (*off*) Oh—it's you.

**Walter** (*off*) Morning, Mrs Ramskill.

**Peggy** (*off*) You'd better leave that thing down here. It's dripping all over. And mind my stockings.

*After a slight pause, Walter appears in a dark suit, looking very uncomfortable*

**Walter** (*sighing*) Eh, what a day. Morning, Mrs Murchinson.

*There is no reaction from Cilla*

*Peggy enters*

**Peggy** If you've come round to see Ethel, well you can't. She's still upstairs getting Alison ready. And that umbrella of yours is ruining the hall carpet.

**Walter** It won't do it no harm. And I've not come round to see anybody.

I've just come out of the way of our Melvyn. (*He sits in the easy chair*)

*Cilla realizes who it is, and at once switches on her hearing-aid again*

**Cilla** Oh, it's you, Walter. I thought it was the Aunts. Just a minute. (*She adjusts the hearing-aid*) That's better. I can hear you now.

**Walter** I'm just saying. I've come round out of our Melvyn's way. He lost a collar stud in the bedroom fifteen minutes ago, and now we've got the carpet up in the living-room. Don't ask me why, because I couldn't begin to explain, but it's all typical Melvyn.

**Peggy** I should have thought you'd have been better off trying to give him a hand to get ready, than coming round here an hour before the wedding.

**Walter** Give him a hand? You must be joking. I want to get to the church in a car—not an ambulance. (*To Cilla*) You know, I still can't understand it. Here they are getting married, and six weeks ago I don't think they'd exchanged more than half a dozen words in the three years they've known each other.

**Cilla** Never mind, Walter. Things are going to work out. You'll see.

**Walter** Aye—but it's really scuttled *my* plans. And I just can't understand what she sees in him.

**Peggy** Well, they do say that love is blind—and we all know that in her case—it's certainly short-sighted.

**Cilla** (*sweetly*) I wonder if you'd mind doing something for me, Mrs Ramskill?

**Peggy** Of course. What is it?

**Cilla** (*tartly*) Shut up.

**Peggy** (*stung*) Well, really. (*She turns to the window*) There's a car outside. A taxi.

*The doorbell chimes*

*Peggy hurries out to the hall to answer it*

**Cilla** (*agitated*) It's the Aunts. (*She fumbles with her hearing-aid*) I'm switching off. Give me a nudge if there's anything I should listen to. (*She switches off*)

**Harry** (*off*) Made it. What a day. Oh—hello.

**Peggy** (*off*) I'll tell Ethel you're here.

**Ethel** (*off, calling*) Is that the dress?

**Harry** (*off*) Sorry I'm late. The car broke down.

**Ethel** (*off*) I'll be right down.

*Harry enters, looking smart but subdued. He carries a large dress box*

*Walter taps Cilla, who looks round, sees Harry, and switches on again*

**Harry** Thought I'd never get here. I'd just left the Studio when the engine stalled. Right in the middle of the High Street. I couldn't move it an inch. Had to get a taxi in the end.

*Ethel enters from the stairs*

**Ethel** Thank goodness you're here. Alison's having hysterics. (*She sees the box*) Is that it?
**Harry** (*handing it over*) That's it.

*Peggy enters from the hall*

**Peggy** Can we have a peep?
**Ethel** There isn't time. We've only got three-quarters of an hour, now. Haven't the Aunts arrived yet?

*Ethel takes the box and exits upstairs*

**Walter** Looks as though things are beginning to liven up around here.
**Cilla** (*beaming*) Ah—but wait till they *really* get started.
**Peggy** (*looking stairwards*) I wonder if I should go up and help?
**Harry** Perhaps *I* had.
**Peggy** (*indignantly*) You certainly won't. You can't go barging into a girl's bedroom when she's getting dressed. Even if you *are* a dress designer.
**Harry** What do you mean—even if I'm a dress designer?
**Peggy** Well. (*She looks round at the others*) We all know about *dress designers*, don't we?
**Cilla** I don't.
**Walter** Me neither.
**Peggy** Well—you don't find many who are—well—married, do you? At least—not to members of the opposite sex.
**Harry** (*quietly*) Are you suggesting that there may be something wrong with me, Mrs—whatever your name is?
**Peggy** I'm not suggesting anything, Mr Elphinstone, but what I always say is—if the cap fits—then wear it.
**Walter** (*rising*) Now just a minute . . .
**Harry** (*waving him to sit again*) It's all right, Mr Thornton. I can deal with this myself. (*To Peggy*) I suppose this came up because I couldn't find time to design the wedding dress for *your* daughter, didn't it?

*Peggy looks flustered*

**Cilla** (*ears pricking*) When was this?
**Harry** Five weeks ago. She turned up at my Oxford studio with her daughter, and asked me to drop everything else I was working on so that I could concentrate on designing and making a wedding gown for *them*. I told her it was impossible and sent them away. Besides, I didn't much like their attitude. (*To Peggy*) Now shall I tell you *why* it was impossible? I *couldn't* design a gown for your daughter that would make her look like a princess. I just haven't got that much talent.
**Peggy** (*stunned*) Well, really . . .
**Cilla** (*chuckling*) You asked for that one, all right.
**Harry** (*to Peggy*) So if you've anything more to say on the subject, you'd better say it now and get it off your chest.

*Ethel hurries down the stairs*

**Ethel** Harry—I wonder if you could come upstairs for a minute and see Alison? She's having a bit of bother with the dress.
**Harry** (*turning*) What kind of bother?
**Ethel** (*on the verge of tears*) She says it doesn't fit.
**Harry** But it *must* do.
**Cilla** Of course it must. She's had enough fittings for it.
**Harry** (*worried*) I'd better have a look at it. (*To Ethel*) Lead the way.
**Ethel** (*leading him out*) We'll have to hurry. The cars will be here in a few minutes. I think it must be something to do with . . . (*Her voice trails off as they go upstairs*)

*Ethel and Harry exit upstairs*

**Peggy** (*spiteful and triumphant*) Doesn't fit her. Did you hear that? It doesn't fit her. So much for the great Mr Harry Elphinstone. Thank goodness I changed my mind about letting him do our Edna's.
**Walter** He'll fix it.
**Peggy** I should think he *will* fix it. All that money. This is what comes of trying to do things in a rush. We've been planning our Edna's wedding for months. She's even having *two* rehearsals for the wedding ceremony.
**Cilla** Oh?
**Peggy** There'll be nothing going wrong at *her* wedding.
**Cilla** Not unless the rehearsals I hear she's been having for her *honeymoon* bear fruit.

*Peggy's face assumes an outraged expression*

*Frank enters from upstairs, in his best suit*

**Frank** Morning, all. Cars arrived yet? (*He glances out of the window*) My, my, my.
**Walter** No sign of it letting up?
**Frank** Nary a one. It's still as black as pitch. Not to worry, though. We'll all be under cover. (*Turning*) Drinks, anybody?
**Cilla** I'll have a gin.
**Frank** No spirits for you, you naughty old lady. Doctor's orders.
**Cilla** Bother the doctor. What's he want to keep me alive for if I'm not allowed to enjoy myself? Make it a large one.
**Frank** (*crossing to the kitchen*) Anyone else?
**Walter** I wouldn't say no to a glass of beer.
**Peggy** Nothing for *me*, thank you. I don't approve of being drunk in church.

*Frank pulls a face and exits into the kitchen*

*Ethel calls from upstairs*

**Ethel** (*off*) Frank. Let the Aunts in, will you? They're coming up the path.

**Walter** (*rising*) I'll do it.

*Walter exits to the hall*

**Cilla** (*calling*) Keep them out till I've turned this off. (*She fiddles with the hearing-aid again*)

**Walter** (*off*) Come in. We saw you coming.

**Cilla** (*muttering*) Yes. But not quite soon enough. (*She switches off her hearing-aid*)

**Walter** (*off*) Take your coats off. You're soaking. Here—let me help.

*Frank enters with two glasses*

**Frank** One large gin—and one beer. (*He hands the gin to Cilla*)

*Honoria and Matilda enter in their wedding finery. Like their former outfits, these too have the authentic ring of the Edwardian period. Walter is behind them*

Ah—just in time. Drinks coming up. What will you have?

*The sisters look at each other*

Gin? Whisky? Brandy? Sherry? Port?

*The sisters nod madly*

Port? Any particular kind? Tawny or Old Crusted?

**Honoria** Any port in a storm.

*Matilda titters*

**Frank** Two ports coming up. (*He hands the beer to Walter*) That's yours. I'll be back in a sec. (*To the Aunts*) Sit yourselves down.

*The Aunts sit on the sofa next to Cilla*

Keep an eye out for the cars, will you, Walter?

*Frank exits to the kitchen*

**Peggy** (*glancing out of the window*) I think there's one coming up the street now. Yes—it's turning in. This is it.

**Walter** That'll be for Melvyn and Harry. I'd better go see if he's found that collar stud yet. (*To Peggy*) You'd better let Harry know.

**Peggy** (*tartly*) After the way he spoke to me? (*She snorts*) I'm telling him nothing. He can wait till Frank comes back in. In any case he's probably still trying to squeeze Alison into his botched-up wedding dress.

*The doorbell chimes*

**Walter**  That'll be the driver. I'll see him on me way out. (*He puts his glass on the coffee-table*) Tell Frank I've gone for Melvyn.

*Walter exits to the hall*

**Matilda** (*picking up the glass*) Waste not, want not. (*She downs the ale in one fell swoop*)

*Ethel enters downstairs*

**Ethel** (*breathlessly*) Is that the first car? Has anybody gone? (*She sees the Aunts*) You'd better go in the next one. You should have been here ages ago. I told you ten o'clock, didn't I? Where's Frank?

*Frank enters with two glasses of port*

**Frank**  Here I am. All present and correct. What's the trouble? (*He goes to the Aunts*)

**Ethel**  Everything. We still haven't got her into the dress, and the car's outside for Melvyn. He'll have to go on his own, and Harry can go with you.

**Frank**  No he can't. I'm going down with Alison, remember? I'm giving her away.

**Ethel**  There'll be nobody giving her away if we can't get this dress on to her. It's at least six sizes too small.

**Peggy** (*to no-one in particular*) What did I tell you?

**Frank** (*soothingly*) Now don't worry. He'll get her into it.

**Ethel**  He can't. It's impossible.

**Honoria**  Where there's a will, there's a way.

**Ethel** (*groaning*) Oh, no. I can't stand any more.

**Frank**  Now look. Calm down and have a drink. It'll do you the world of good. Steady your nerves.

**Ethel**  It's not my nerves I'm bothered about. It's the dress.

**Frank**  There's nothing wrong with the dress. It's fabulous.

**Ethel** (*her voice rising*) What's the good of it being fabulous if she can't get into it?

**Matilda**  Fine feathers do not make fine birds.

**Frank** (*to Ethel*) Now just you sit in the easy chair for a minute and I'll get you a good, stiff brandy. (*He moves towards the kitchen*)

**Cilla** (*spotting him move*) If you're going for more drinks, you can top this up. (*She waves her glass*)

*Walter enters from the hall, looking puzzled*

**Walter**  Has anybody seen Melvyn? He seems to have vanished.

**Ethel**  Vanished? (*She sinks into the easy chair, exhausted*)

**Walter**  I can't find hair nor hide of him.

**Honoria** Seek and ye shall find.

**Walter** I've *been* seeking—but he's gone. The house is empty.

**Frank** (*shrugging*) He's probably popped out for a breath of air.

**Walter** In this lot? And in any case—he hasn't got time. The car's waiting for him.

**Ethel** (*rising determinedly*) The other one's due in a minute. We'd better let the Aunts go in this one, and send Melvyn in the next.

**Walter** If I can find him.

**Ethel** (*distraught*) I knew it. I *knew* it. Everything's going wrong.

**Frank** Come on, Aunts. Into the car with you.

**Ethel** Where can he have got to?

**Peggy** Well, at the risk of having my head snapped off, I could tell you what *I* think. I think he's got cold feet and made a run for it.

**Walter** Don't talk so daft.

**Peggy** He wouldn't be the first one to do it, and he certainly won't be the last. He might be halfway to London by now.

**Matilda** (*rising*) There's many a true word spoken in jest.

**Ethel** He wouldn't leave her like that without a word. Not Melvyn.

**Frank** Of course he wouldn't. (*He ushers the Aunts towards the arch*) I've told you. He's probably just nipped out for some cigarettes, or something.

*Harry appears in the arch*

**Harry** She's coming down.

**Ethel** (*her face lighting*) You've done it. (*She sighs with relief*) Thank goodness for that.

**Peggy** Well, all I hope is that it's been worth waiting for.

**Harry** Would you mind if she had a few words with her mother first? In private.

**Walter** Private? Oh—no. No, of course not.

**Frank** (*to the Aunts*) Come on, sweethearts. Off you go. We'll see you again in a few minutes.

*Frank exits with Matilda and Honoria*

**Harry** (*to Peggy*) You—er—you could wait in the front room—(*he looks at Ethel*)—if that's all right?

**Ethel** Of course.

**Cilla** (*fiddling with her hearing-aid switch*) What was that? What did you say?

**Ethel** He said you could wait in the front room. Alison wants to have a few words with me—in private.

**Cilla** Yes. Yes, I thought she might. Cutting it a bit fine, though, isn't she? (*She rises*)

*Walter hurries to assist Cilla to the parlour*

Don't rush me. Don't rush me.

*Walter and Cilla exit to the parlour*

**Peggy** (*to Harry*) And what about you?
**Harry** She wants me here as well.
**Peggy** (*sniffing*) I see.

*Peggy exits to the parlour*

**Harry** (*moving back under the arch and calling*) It's all right now, Alison.

*Alison appears in the arch. She is dressed in her old clothes, and her hair is a mess. Her eyes are red with weeping. She moves slowly in*

**Ethel** (*dismayed*) Alison . . .! (*She looks from Alison to Harry then back to Alison again*) Your dress—where is it? (*To Harry*) You said you'd fixed it.
**Harry** No. You assumed that. I just said she was coming down.
**Ethel** You mean—it won't fit at all?
**Harry** Not a hope.
**Ethel** (*frantically*) But why? Why won't it? She must have had a dozen fittings. It's *got* to fit her.
**Alison** (*on the verge of tears again*) It won't. It never would.
**Ethel** I—I don't understand. (*She looks from one to the other*)
**Alison** (*gulping*) I never went for the fittings.
**Ethel** (*dazed*) What?
**Harry** Never turned up for any of them.
**Ethel** But—but . . . (*She looks at Alison appealingly*)
**Alison** I just couldn't. After Harry took my measurements that first day, I felt so ashamed of the size I was, I convinced myself that he'd never be able to do anything, and I hadn't the courage to go to the Studio. Every time I told you I was going for a fitting, I just went into town and stuffed myself silly on anything I could lay my hands on. I've put on a stone and a half in the last six weeks. That's why the dress won't fit me.
**Ethel** (*to Harry*) But why didn't you tell us she wasn't coming to you? You could have told Frank and he'd have been able to do something about it.
**Alison** Don't blame him, Mum. I asked him not to say anything.
**Ethel** Why? What on earth for? What was the point?
**Alison** I don't want to go through with it. I don't want to marry Melvyn. (*She begins to cry again*)
**Ethel** Oh, Alison. (*She puts her arms around Alison*)
**Harry** I've tried to talk her round. I thought it was just pre-wedding nerves—but it's not.
**Alison** (*sobbing*) I don't love him, Mum. It wouldn't be fair to him.
**Ethel** (*gently*) You've picked a fine time to find that out, love. On your wedding day.
**Alison** (*still sobbing*) I know.

**Ethel** What are we going to do? All those people down there at the church, and the reception waiting.

**Alison** I'm sorry.

**Ethel** No. No, don't be sorry. Better to have thought about it now—even at this stage—than to think about it when it's too late.

**Harry** There's something else . . .

**Ethel** Yes—I've just thought of it. How could you have tried to talk her round? You've only been up there with her for five minutes. You haven't had time.

**Alison** (*sniffling*) Yes, he has. I've been seeing him quite a lot this last two weeks.

**Ethel** (*puzzled*) But you said . . .

**Alison** I said I hadn't been to his Studio. (*She sniffles*) He rang me up at the Exchange five weeks ago to find out why I hadn't been for the first fitting. I told him I'd forgotten and promised to go the week after, but I didn't—and he rang me again. I gave him another excuse—and another—and another—until finally I had to agree to meet him to stop him telling you and Uncle Frank about it. That's when I realized I needed somebody to talk to about it all. To tell them how scared I was, and what a big mistake it had turned out to be.

**Ethel** You could have talked to *me*, love. I'd have understood.

**Alison** No. It had to be someone outside the family. A stranger. Anyway—it was Harry I told. Harry who listened—and it's Harry I've fallen in love with. (*She sobs again*)

**Ethel** (*dismayed*) Oh, no.

**Harry** Sorry, Mrs Murchinson. But I feel the same way about Alison, too.

**Ethel** But you can't do—I mean . . . (*Weakly*) You can't.

**Harry** I know—but I do. We've tried to do the right thing. Alison to go through with a wedding she didn't want, and myself to keep quiet and do nothing to create problems—but well—she just couldn't do it.

**Ethel** (*helplessly*) I—I think we'd better call Walter in.

**Alison** (*aghast*) Oh, Mum!

**Ethel** I know—but he'll have to be told. After all—it's his son you're leaving at the altar.

**Harry** Would you like me to—tell him? It might be better.

**Ethel** It's all right—Harry. I think a woman's approach is better with things like this. Would—would you ask him to come in?

*Harry moves to the parlour door and calls*

**Harry** Mr Thornton.

**Alison** (*moving towards the window*) Poor Melvyn.

*Walter appears at the parlour door*

**Walter** Want me? (*He sees Alison, and reacts*)

**Ethel** Come in, Walter.

*Walter moves into the room*

You'd better sit down. I—I've got something to tell you.

**Walter** (*looking at all the strained faces*) It's not Melvyn, is it? There's nothing happened to him?

**Harry** No—no. It's nothing like that, Mr Thornton. Sit down, will you?

*Walter sits on the sofa, warily*

**Ethel** (*uncertain of where to start*) It's about the wedding.

**Walter** Aye?

**Harry** I'm afraid it's off.

**Ethel** (*quickly*) She—she doesn't want to go through with it.

**Alison** (*turning*) It's not because I've got anything against him, Mr Thornton, because I haven't—but—well—I'm not in love with him.

**Walter** (*after a short pause*) I see. And how long have you felt like this, then?

**Alison** (*miserably*) Ever since the day he proposed to me. I should never have accepted him, should I?

**Walter** (*quietly*) And you've never thought to mention it to him?

**Alison** Of course I have. Dozens of times. But I didn't know *how*. I wasn't too sure about it myself—and he's so much in love with me for some reason—I just couldn't bring myself to hurt him. Don't you understand?

**Walter** But you'll leave him standing at the altar today, though? You don't think *that* will hurt him?

*Alison looks away in despair*

**Harry** Surely it's better for him to find out now—before it's too late, than for him to go through the rest of his life in misery because of a wedding that nobody wants?

**Walter** How do you mean—nobody?

**Harry** Well isn't it obvious? Alison doesn't want it—and if it's going to make *her* unhappy, then Mrs Murchinson doesn't want it either. (*More quietly*) And *I* certainly don't want it.

**Walter** Oh? And why's that?

**Ethel** (*taking a deep breath*) He's in love with her, Walter. They want to get married.

**Walter** (*heavily*) I see.

**Alison** (*brokenly*) I'm sorry, Mr Thornton.

**Walter** You're not half as sorry as me, lass. Not half as sorry.

**Harry** But you must be able to see that she's doing the right thing, Mr Thornton.

**Walter** Right thing by who? I'm sorry, Alison, but I don't see how you can call it off at this stage. Not now. It'll break that lad's heart. You're the first girl who's ever looked twice at him.

**Harry** But if she doesn't, then it's going to break *her* heart.

**Walter** (*heavily*) Aye.

**Ethel** There must be something we can do, Walter.

**Walter** (*shaking his head*) It's up to Alison. Either she goes upstairs and gets herself ready—or else somebody had better get down to that church and tell everybody to go home. (*He looks at Alison*) Which is it going to be, love?

**Alison** (*after a long pause*) I'll go and get ready.

**Ethel** (*dazed*) But you've nothing to wear.

**Alison** I'll find something. (*She smiles sadly at Harry*) I'm sorry, Harry.

**Harry** (*gently*) It's all right. (*He turns away*)

*Alison exits slowly upstairs*

**Ethel** I'd better go with her.

*Ethel hurries out after Alison*

**Harry** I suppose it might be best if I went as well.

**Walter** (*nodding*) Perhaps it would, lad—under the circumstances. (*He rises*) I'm sorry things had to happen this way—but—well—that's how life is, I'm afraid. Nothing works out exactly the way we'd like it to, does it?

**Harry** (*forcing a smile*) I suppose not. (*He holds out his hand*) Well—good-bye, Mr Thornton.

**Walter** (*shaking it*) Good-bye, Harry. Better luck next time, eh?

**Harry** (*glancing out of the window*) Looks like the second car's arrived.

**Walter** (*looking*) Aye. I'd best get Mrs Murchinson out to it. (*He goes to the parlour door and calls*) Second car.

**Harry** Would you like a hand with her? Down to the gate.

**Walter** I wouldn't say no.

*Cilla and Peggy enter from the parlour*

**Cilla** Where's Alison? (*She peers around*)

**Walter** She—er—she's gone back upstairs to finish dressing.

*Cilla frowns*

**Peggy** Well, she'll have to get a move on. She's not got much time left.

**Walter** (*to Cilla*) I'll get your coat. (*He turns to the arch*)

*Frank and the Aunts enter through the arch*

**Frank** The blasted car won't start. We've been standing out there for ages. The driver's just gone for another. Melvyn turned up, yet?

**Harry** Not yet.

**Frank** Well, you may as well all sit down again until the next car arrives. I'll fix some drinks.

*Cilla sits in the easy chair, the Aunts on the sofa with Peggy. Walter and Harry stand*

Now—who wants what?

*Melvyn enters from the hall, in his wedding suit*

**Walter** Melvyn! Where the devil have you been?

**Melvyn** (*taken aback*) In town. At the solicitor's. Why? Am I late?

**Frank** Late? You're due there ten minutes ago. (*He grins*) But don't worry. It looks like we're all going to be late. The car's broken down.

**Walter** (*to Melvyn*) And what were you doing down at the solicitor's? You've not been making your will out, have you?

**Melvyn** No.

**Walter** And anyway—it's Saturday. They're not open.

**Melvyn** This one was. They opened it especially for me. I got this letter from them, you see. Asking me to go down there. So I made an appointment with them for today.

**Peggy** On your wedding morning?

**Melvyn** Well—I thought I'd have time.

**Walter** You didn't.

**Melvyn** They wanted to give me this. (*He takes a manilla envelope out of his pocket*)

**Cilla** (*peering*) What is it?

**Melvyn** It's a cheque—for two thousand pounds.

*Everybody reacts*

**Walter** (*stunned*) For what?

**Melvyn** Knocking the *Horse and Groom* down. Well—not exactly for knocking it down—but—well—for knocking it down.

**Walter** (*exasperated*) Melvyn . . . !

**Melvyn** You see—the brewery had been trying to get it knocked down for years, so they could use the site to build a bigger one. But with it being an Ancient Monument, well—they couldn't do anything about it except to go on paying out thousands of pounds to keep it standing. They said it was absolutely riddled with death-watch beetle, and they were tickled to bits when I knocked it down by accident—the brewers that is—not the death-watch beetles—because it's saved them a fortune. So they've sent me this cheque.

**Peggy** But that's criminal.

**Melvyn** No it isn't. They said the money was for damages I might be able to claim against them for my injuries.

**Walter** (*stunned*) Well I'm blowed.

**Frank** (*laughing with delight*) Now that's what I call a real turn up for the books. Two thousand pounds. You'll be able to use that as a deposit for a house of your own.

**Melvyn** (*uneasily*) Er—yes. (*He looks down at the floor in discomfort*)

**Frank** All we have to do is find you a few more places to demolish, and you can set up in business. You'll be a millionaire in no time.

**Melvyn** (*still looking down*) There's something else I've got to tell you—about the wedding.

**Cilla** Yes?

**Melvyn** Well—I can't go through with it. I don't want to get married.

*Everyone reacts*

It was all a mistake, you see, and I shouldn't have asked her to marry me, but I thought I was doing it for the best and now I've realized I wasn't and I don't want to go through with it.

**Frank** (*amazed*) What do you mean—you thought you were doing it for the best?

**Melvyn** (*squirming*) Well—that was what you wanted me to do, wasn't it?

**Frank** (*startled*) Eh? But I never said a word.

**Melvyn** You remember that day I came round here to show you my new glue, and it got stuck to the chair and everything? Well, after my dad marched me out of here—I came back for my brush and to say I was sorry for everything—and I overheard you talking.

**Frank** (*aghast*) You mean—you were out there in the hall?

**Melvyn** (*nodding*) I heard everything. How Alison felt, and what people were saying. And I thought that if *I* offered to marry her, well at least she'd have the pleasure of being able to turn me down, and it'd make her feel good. But it didn't work out that way at all because she accepted me.

**Harry** But you told her that you were in love with her.

**Melvyn** What else do you think I *could* tell her?

**Frank** And you're not?

**Melvyn** (*miserably*) No.

**Walter** And you never have been?

**Melvyn** No.

**Harry** But that's *marvellous*.

**Melvyn**
**Peggy** } Eh? { (*Speaking together*)
**Frank**

**Harry** (*to Melvyn*) So you want to call the wedding off?

**Melvyn** (*baffled*) Yes.

**Walter** (*grimly*) Then why the devil didn't you say something before, you great daft lump?

**Melvyn** Well, I'd heard about all the money they'd been spending on it, and I daren't say anything because it would all have been wasted, and maybe they'd have sued me, or something—and after what you threatened if I did anything wrong again . . . But now I've got this cheque, I can pay for everything myself, can't I? All I've got to do is break the news to Alison. (*Depressed*) Oh, lor.

**Harry** Melvyn—you're *wonderful*! (*He grabs him and kisses him with glee*)

**Peggy** (*outraged*) What did I tell you?

**Harry** I'll break the news to her myself.

*Harry dashes off upstairs*

**Frank** Would somebody please tell me what's going on around here?

**Cilla** Oh, use your eyes, Frank. They've both come to their senses and called the wedding off.

**Frank** Both?

**Cilla** Of course, both. They're not in love. Never have been. *I've* known that for weeks. She's fallen for your friend Elph.

**Peggy** (*snorting*) Fairy's more like it.

**Melvyn** (*surprised*) You mean—she won't mind?

**Cilla** Of course she won't mind. She'll be delighted.

**Peggy** Jilted on her wedding day—and she'll be delighted.

**Cilla** Yes, but not half so delighted as you, Mrs Ramskill. I can read your mind like a book. You think that now this wedding's off, your Edna stands a chance of getting a look in with that competition, don't you?

**Peggy** I haven't even given it a thought.

**Cilla** Good. Because I don't think she'll stand a chance in any case.

**Peggy** (*bridling*) And why not?

**Cilla** Because if I'm any judge of character—there'll be an even bigger event taking place in the next few weeks.

*Ethel and Harry enter hurriedly downstairs*

**Ethel** Melvyn. Is it true?

**Melvyn** I'm ever so sorry.

**Ethel** (*hugging him*) You don't have to be sorry about anything, love. It's the best bit of news we've had in months.

**Melvyn** Where's Alison?

**Ethel** She'll be right down. Oh, Walter. (*She moves to him in relief*)

**Cilla** *I* think this calls for a celebratory drink, Frank.

*The doorbell chimes*

**Walter** That'll be the other car.

*Alison, wrapped in a dressing-gown, enters hurriedly downstairs*

**Alison** (*hugging Melvyn*) Melvyn.

**Melvyn** You don't mind? Honestly? You don't hate me?

**Alison** Of course I don't hate you. I love you. (*She kisses him*)

**Harry** Eh?

**Alison** In the nicest way. (*She moves to Harry and they embrace*)

**Frank** Well—this is all very touching, I'm sure—but there's a car waiting outside, and a couple of hundred people down at the church—not to mention a reception at the Tudor Hall.

**Harry** Don't worry about the reception. It won't be wasted. We'll have it as an engagement party for Alison and myself. I'll foot the bill.

**Frank** And what about the tickets for the Canary Islands?

**Cilla** Give 'em to Honoria and Matilda. I'll pay for *them*. It'll be worth it for the peace. (*She beams at the Aunts*)

**Walter** So that's it, then, is it? All sorted out.

**Cilla** Not quite, Walter. Isn't there something *you'd* like to say?

**Walter** (*frowning*) Me? What is there for me to say?

**Cilla** I could think of a thousand and one things—but just for the minute, I'll have to content myself by pointing *this* out. Now that your Melvyn isn't going to marry our Alison—there's nothing in the world to stop you from proposing to her mother.

**Ethel** (*shocked*) Aunt Cilla . . .

**Cilla** Aunt Cilla nothing. (*To Walter*) Well—go on, man. You've been dying to do it for the last year, haven't you? Well, now's your chance.

**Ethel** (*highly embarrassed*) I'm sure he's been doing nothing of the kind, Aunt Cilla, so please drop the subject. You're embarrassing the poor man.

**Cilla** Rubbish. (*To Walter*) Isn't it? Well?

**Walter** Well . . . (*He looks round at the sea of faces*)

**Cilla** Go on. She won't bite you.

**Ethel** (*firmly*) That's quite enough. Now somebody answer that door. That poor car driver will be soaked. (*No-one moves*) Frank . . .

**Walter** Ethel . . . (*He looks at her*)

*The door chimes ring out again*

**Ethel** I'll go myself. (*She turns*)

**Walter** Will you?

*Ethel freezes*

**Ethel** (*turning slowly*) Will I—what?

**Walter** You know—marry me?

*There is an agonized silence*

**Cilla** You can't live on memories for ever.

*Silence*

**Alison** Mother?

*Ethel looks at her*

**Walter** Well?

**Ethel** (*looking at him again*) I—I . . . (*Her eyes blinking*) Yes.

*There are delighted gasps all round*

**Walter** (*going to her*) Ethel.

*Ethel and Walter embrace*

**Cilla** (*triumphantly*) That's better. Now somebody go and answer that door.

**Melvyn** I'll do it.

*Melvyn exits quickly to the hall*

**Frank** (*calling*) Melvyn! Wait! The umbrellas . . .!

*There is a yell from Melvyn and a huge crash off*

(*Groaning*) There goes the hallstand again.

*Frank exits to the hall*

**Walter** Well, as Mrs Murchinson said a few minutes ago—I think this calls for a celebration drink.
**Harry** I'll do it.

*Harry exits to the kitchen*

**Ethel** (*with a nervous laugh*) I've gone all shaky at the knees.
**Walter** Me too. I never expected I'd have to propose in a crowded room. (*He smiles at Ethel*) But it was worth it.

*Melvyn enters, holding his eye*

**Melvyn** It's going to be a beauty by tomorrow. (*He winces*)

*Frank enters in his overcoat*

**Frank** I'm just on my way to church to let everybody know what's happened. I'll meet you all at the reception rooms in about an hour. O.K.?
**Peggy** I think I'd better come with you, if you don't mind. (*She rises*) If I stay here much longer, I might find *myself* getting a divorce and marrying *you*. (*She laughs*)

*Harry enters with a tray and a bottle of champagne and glasses. Some are already filled*

**Harry** Don't go before you've had a drink. (*He hands the glasses round*)
**Cilla** Everybody served? Then here's a toast. To Ethel and Alison. The two best brides of *any* year.

*The toasts are drunk*

**Walter** Here—and what about the Aunts? They haven't said a dicky-bird since they came back in. (*To the Aunts*) Isn't there anything *you* want to say?

*The Aunts look at each other and smile. Then they both stand simultaneously and raise their glasses*

**Honoria**⎫
**Matilda**⎭ All's well that ends well. ⎰ (*Speaking together*)

*Everyone laughs and echoes the toast, as—*

the CURTAIN *falls*

# FURNITURE AND PROPERTY LIST

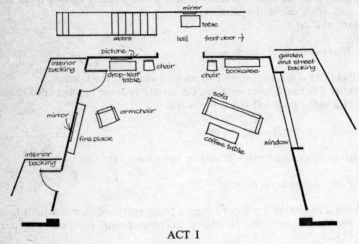

## ACT I

### SCENE 1

*On stage:*   Sofa. *On it:* cushions
Armchair. *On it:* cushion
2 dining-chairs (one with rip-off seat)
Oval drop-leaf table. *On it:* runner, vase of flowers
Coffee-table. *On it:* tray with coffee-cup, saucer, plate of assorted biscuits
Hall table. *On it:* bowl of dried flowers and ferns. *Over it:* oval, gold-rimmed mirror
Small bookcase. *In it:* books. *On top:* magazine, table lamp
*On wall above oval table:* print of Old Master
*On mantelpiece:* assorted ornaments. *Above it:* mirror
Net curtains
Heavy curtains
Carpet

*Off stage:*   Coffee-pot **(Ethel)**
Cup and saucer **(Ethel)**
Bunch of flowers **(Walter)**
Cup and saucer **(Ethel)**
Lunch-box with sandwiches, wrapped box of chocolates **(Frank)**
Plate of sandwiches **(Ethel)**
Local newspaper **(Alison)**
Tray with 3 cups, 3 saucers, 3 small plates, milk jug, sugar bowl, spoons, teapot **(Ethel)**

SCENE 2

*Strike:*    All coffee things, plate of biscuits
            Lunch-box
            Sandwiches
            Newspaper
            Tea-tray and cups

*Set:*      Room tidy

*Off stage:*  Large carpet-bag with embroidery-rings and silks **(Honoria)**
            Large carpet-bag with embroidery-rings and silks **(Matilda)**
            Tray with 4 cups, 4 saucers, 4 side plates, milk jug, sugar bowl, tea-
               spoons **(Ethel)**
            Teapot **(Ethel)**
            Large dirty paintbrush **(Melvyn)**
            Folded sketch **(Harry)**
            Tray of crockery **(Ethel)**

ACT II

SCENE 1

*Strike:*    Tea things

*Set:*      Room tidy

*Off stage:*  **Frank's shoes (Alison)**
            **Frank's shirt (Alison)**
            Tray of used tea things **(Honoria)**
            Tray with 4 cups, 4 saucers, plates, teaspoons, milk jug, sugar bowl
               **(Ethel)**
            Teapot **(Ethel)**
            Bowl of water **(Ethel)**
            Sweater and slacks **(Frank)**

*Personal:*  **Cilla:** walking-stick, hearing-aid
            **Walter:** bandage, sling
            **Melvyn:** handkerchief
            **Alison:** wig

SCENE 2

*Strike:*    2 trays of tea things

*Set:*      Various brightly wrapped boxes and parcels on tables
            Wedding cards on mantelpiece

*Off stage:*  Large dress box **(Harry)**
            Glass of gin **(Frank)**
            Glass of beer **(Frank)**
            2 glasses of port **(Frank)**
            Cheque in manilla envelope **(Melvyn)**
            Tray with opened bottle of champagne and 10 glasses, some of them
               filled **(Harry)**

# LIGHTING PLOT

Property fittings required: wall brackets, centre light, hall pendant, table lamp
Interior.   A living-room. The same scene throughout

ACT I, Scene 1.   Day

*To open:*  General effect of bright sunshine. Fire lit

*No cues*


ACT I, Scene 1.   Day

*To open:*  As Scene 1

*No cues*


ACT II, Scene 1.   Evening

*To open:*  All interior lighting on. Fire lit

*No cues*


ACT II, Scene 2.   Morning

*To open:*  Very dark exterior. Centre light on. Fire lit

Cue 1    As Curtain rises                                        (Page 59)
        *Lightning—continue intermittently until scene established*

# EFFECTS PLOT

## ACT I
### SCENE 1

Cue 1 **Alison** sits to drink tea                                    (Page 14)
*Doorbell chimes*

### SCENE 2

Cue 2 **Ethel:** "Really, Alison . . ."                              (Page 19)
*Doorbell chimes*

Cue 3 **Walter:** ". . . got me at it as well."                      (Page 23)
*Doorbell chimes*

Cue 4 **Alison:** "Melvyn . . .!"                                    (Page 24)
*Loud crash*

Cue 5 After **Ethel** exits to kitchen                               (Page 33)
*Loud crash of crockery*

## ACT II
### SCENE 1

Cue 6 **Frank:** ". . . about it some day, can't we?"               (Page 39)
*Doorbell chimes*

Cue 7 **Frank:** ". . . by the door . . ."                          (Page 55)
*Loud crash*

### SCENE 2

Cue 8 As CURTAIN rises                                               (Page 59)
*Heavy rain, occasional distant thunder*

Cue 9 **Ethel** exits upstairs                                      (Page 62)
*Doorbell chimes*

Cue 10 **Peggy:** "A taxi."                                          (Page 63)
*Doorbell chimes*

Cue 11 **Peggy:** ". . . botched-up wedding dress."                 (Page 66)
*Doorbell chimes*

Cue 12 **Cilla:** ". . . a celebratory drink, Frank."               (Page 75)
*Doorbell chimes*

Cue 13 **Walter:** "Ethel . . ."                                     (Page 76)
*Doorbell chimes*

Cue 14 **Frank:** "The umbrellas . . .!"                             (Page 76)
*Loud crash*